W9-BRS-707

Gretchen Bitterlin
Dennis Johnson
Donna Price
Sylvia Ramirez
K. Lynn Savage, Series Editor

Ventures 4

STUDENT'S BOOK

Removed from
Media Center
Collection
WITHLACOOCHEE TECHNICAL INSTITUTE
1201 W. Main Street
INVERNESS, FL 34450-4696

CAMBRIDGE
UNIVERSITY PRESS

CAMBRIDGE UNIVERSITY PRESS
Cambridge, New York, Melbourne, Madrid, Cape Town, Singapore,
São Paulo, Delhi, Dubai, Tokyo, Mexico City

Cambridge University Press
32 Avenue of the Americas, New York, NY 10013–2473, USA

www.cambridge.org
Information on this title: www.cambridge.org/9780521600989

© Cambridge University Press 2008

This publication is in copyright. Subject to statutory exception
and to the provisions of relevant collective licensing agreements,
no reproduction of any part may take place without the written
permission of Cambridge University Press.

First published 2008
7th printing 2010

Printed in the United States of America

A catalog record for this publication is available from the British Library.

ISBN 978-0-521-60098-9 pack consisting of Student's Book and Audio CD
ISBN 978-0-521-67961-9 Workbook
ISBN 978-0-521-72105-9 pack consisting of Teacher's Edition and Teacher's Toolkit Audio CD / CD-ROM
ISBN 978-0-521-67732-5 CDs (Audio)
ISBN 978-0-521-67733-2 Cassettes
ISBN 978-0-521-67586-4 Add Ventures

Cambridge University Press has no responsibility for
the persistence or accuracy of URLs for external or
third-party Internet Web sites referred to in this publication
and does not guarantee that any content on such
Web sites is, or will remain, accurate or appropriate.

Art direction, book design, photo research, and layout services: Adventure House, NYC

Authors' acknowledgments

The authors would like to acknowledge and thank focus group participants and reviewers for their insightful comments, as well as CUP editorial, marketing, and production staffs, whose thorough research and attention to detail have resulted in a quality product.

The publishers would also like to extend their particular thanks to the following reviewers and consultants for their valuable insights and suggestions:

Francesca Armendaris, North Orange County Community College District, Anaheim, California; **Alex A. Baez**, The Texas Professional Development Group, Austin, Texas; **Kit Bell**, LAUSD Division of Adult and Career Education, Los Angeles, California; **Rose Anne Cleary**, Catholic Migration Office, Diocese of Brooklyn, Brooklyn, New York; **Inga Cristi**, Pima Community College Adult Education, Tucson, Arizona; **Kay De Gennaro**, West Valley Occupational Center, Woodland Hills, California; **Patricia DeHesus-Lopez**, Illinois Community College Board, Springfield, Illinois; **Magali Apareaida Morais Duignan**, Augusta State University, Augusta, Georgia; **Gayle Fagan**, Harris County Department of Education, Houston, Texas; **Lisa A. Fears**, Inglewood Community Adult School, Inglewood, California; **Jas Gill**, English Language Institute at the University of British Columbia, Vancouver, British Columbia, Canada; **Elisabeth Goodwin**, Pima Community College Adult Education, Tucson, Arizona; **Carolyn Grimaldi**, Center for Immigrant Education and Training, LaGuardia Community College, Long Island City, New York; **Masha Gromyko**, Pima Community College Adult Education, Tucson, Arizona; **Jennifer M. Herrin**, Albuquerque TVI Community College, Albuquerque, New Mexico; **Giang T. Hoang**, Evans Community Adult School, Los Angeles, California; **Karen Hribar**, LAUSD West Valley Occupational Center, Los Angeles, California; **Patricia Ishill**, Union County College, Union County, New Jersey; **Dr. Stephen G. Karel**, McKinley Community School for Adults, Honolulu, Hawaii; **Aaron Kelly**, North Orange County Community College District, Anaheim, California; **Dan Kiernan**, Metro Skills Center, LAUSD, Los Angeles, California; **Kirsten Kilcup**, Green River Community College, Auburn, Washington; **Tom Knutson**, New York Association for New Americans, Inc., New York, New York; **Liz Koenig-Golombek**, LAUSD, Los Angeles, California; **Anita Lemonis**, West Valley Occupational Center, Los Angeles, California; **Lia Lerner**, Burbank Adult School, Burbank, California; **Susan Lundquist**, Pima Community College Adult Education, Tucson, Arizona; **Dr. Amal Mahmoud**, Highline Community College, Des Moines, Washington; **Fatiha Makloufi**, Hostos Community College, Bronx, New York; **Judith Martin-Hall**, Indian River Community College, Fort Pierce, Florida; **Gwen Mayer**, Van Nuys Community Adult School, Los Angeles, California; **Lois Miller**, Pima Community College Adult Education, Tucson, Arizona; **Vicki Moore**, El Monte-Rosemead Adult School, El Monte, California; **Jeanne Petrus-Rivera**, Cuyahoga Community College, Cleveland, Ohio; **Pearl W. Pigott**, Houston Community College, Houston, Texas; **Catherine Porter**, Adult Learning Resource Center, Des Plaines, Illinois; **Planaria Price**, Evans Community Adult School, Los Angeles, California; **James P. Regan**, NYC Board of Education, New York, New York; **Catherine M. Rifkin**, Florida Community College at Jacksonville, Jacksonville, Florida; **Amy Schneider**, Pacoima Skills Center, Los Angeles, California; **Bonnie Sherman**, Green River Community College, Auburn, Washington; **Julie Singer**, Garfield Community Adult School, Los Angeles, California; **Yilin Sun**, Seattle Central Community College, Seattle, Washington; **André Sutton**, Belmont Community Adult School, Los Angeles, California; **Deborah Thompson**, El Camino Real Community Adult School, Los Angeles, California; **Evelyn Trottier**, Basic Studies Division, Seattle Central Community College, Seattle, Washington; **Debra Un**, New York University, American Language Institute, New York, New York; **Jodie Morgan Vargas**, Orange County Public Schools, Orlando, Florida; **Christopher Wahl**, Hudson County Community College, Jersey City, New Jersey; **Ethel S. Watson**, Evans Community Adult School, Los Angeles, California; **Barbara Williams**; **Mimi Yang**, Belmont Community Adult School, Los Angeles, California; **Adèle Youmans**, Pima Community College Adult Education, Tucson, Arizona.

Scope and sequence

UNIT TITLE TOPIC	FUNCTIONS	LISTENING AND SPEAKING	VOCABULARY	GRAMMAR FOCUS
Welcome Unit pages 2–5	• Exchanging information • Making introductions • Discussing study habits and strategies for studying	• Asking about personality types • Asking about likes and dislikes • Introducing a classmate	• Personality traits • Activities • Study habits and strategies	• Verb tense review: present, present continuous, past, present perfect, present perfect continuous, past continuous, and future with *be going to*
Unit 1 **Personal information** pages 6–17 Topic: **Ways to be smart**	• Describing personal strengths • Expressing opinions • Expressing agreement and disagreement	• Asking about aptitudes • Discussing multiple intelligences • Giving opinions	• Adjectives and adverbs • Multiple intelligences • Prefixes and roots	• Noun clauses with *that* • Contrasting adjectives and adverbs
Unit 2 **At school** pages 18–29 Topic: **Planning for success**	• Inquiring about educational opportunities • Describing educational goals • Describing successful people	• Asking about courses and classes • Discussing how to continue one's education • Discussing obstacles and successes	• Education and careers • Educational requirements • Making vocabulary cards	• The present passive • Infinitives after passive verbs
Review: Units 1 and 2 pages 30–31		• Understanding a conversation		
Unit 3 **Friends and family** pages 32–43 Topic: **Parents and children**	• Discussing appropriate behaviors at home and school • Using polite forms of language • Expressing agreement and disagreement	• Asking about rules at home and at school • Asking questions indirectly • Talking about past events and experiences	• Rules and expectations • Word families	• Indirect *Wh-* questions • Indirect *Yes / No* questions
Unit 4 **Health** pages 44–55 Topic: **Stressful situations**	• Discussing stress • Expressing necessity and lack of necessity • Making suggestions • Expressing past regrets	• Asking about stress • Discussing ways to cope with stress • Giving advice about past actions	• Stress and how to cope • Suffixes	• *ought to, shouldn't, have to, don't have to* • *should have, shouldn't have*
Review: Units 3 and 4 pages 56–57		• Understanding a phone conversation		
Unit 5 **Around town** pages 58–69 Topic: **Community involvement**	• Describing volunteer responsibilities • Describing a sequence of events • Describing repeated actions in the past and present	• Asking about volunteer activities • Discussing personal experiences of volunteering or helping people • Discussing schedules	• Volunteerism • Positive and negative words	• Clauses with *until* and *as soon as* • Repeated actions in the present and past

READING	WRITING	LIFE SKILLS	PRONUNCIATION
• Reading a paragraph about an accident	• Writing sentences about your partner	• Discussing study habits and strategies for learning English	• Pronouncing key vocabulary
• Reading an article about multiple intelligences • Skimming to predict what a reading is about	• Writing a descriptive paragraph about a primary intelligence • Using a topic sentence and supporting details	• Using a dictionary • Reading and understanding a visual diagram	• Pronouncing key vocabulary
• Reading an article about an immigrant family • Scanning to find specific information	• Writing a descriptive paragraph about a successful person • Using specific details such as facts, examples, and reasons	• Using a dictionary • Reading and understanding a chart about the location of vocational classes	• Pronouncing key vocabulary
			• -ed verb endings
• Reading an article about barriers between generations • Paying attention to words that repeat to get an idea of what a reading is about	• Writing an expository paragraph about a difference between generations • Using transition words to show relationships	• Using a dictionary • Reading and understanding a bar graph • Interpreting a survey of student behaviors	• Pronouncing key vocabulary
• Reading an article about stress • Relating personal experience to the content of a reading	• Writing a descriptive paragraph about how to cope with stress • Using actions and results to organize a paragraph	• Reading and understanding a bar graph • Discussing stress in the workplace	• Pronouncing key vocabulary
			• Contrasting intonation of direct and indirect questions
• Reading an article about volunteers • Using context to guess if the meaning of a word is positive or negative	• Writing a descriptive paragraph about someone who made a difference • Making writing more interesting by including details that answer questions	• Reading and understanding ads for volunteer positions • Discussing volunteer activities	• Pronouncing key vocabulary

UNIT TITLE TOPIC	FUNCTIONS	LISTENING AND SPEAKING	VOCABULARY	GRAMMAR FOCUS
Unit 6 **Time** pages 70–81 Topic: **Time and technology**	• Expressing agreement and disagreement • Giving opinions and reasons	• Talking about time-saving devices • Discussing the advantages and disadvantages of technology	• Technology and time-saving devices • Words with multiple definitions	• *although, even though* • Contrasting *because* and *although*
Review: Units 5 and 6 pages 82–83		• Understanding a radio interview		
Unit 7 **Shopping** pages 84–95 Topic: **Buying and returning merchandise**	• Explaining problems with a purchase • Discussing preferences • Explaining mistakes • Asking for information about store policies	• Asking about returning merchandise • Asking about store policies • Talking about shopping mistakes • Identifying store personnel • Describing people, places, and things	• Buying and returning merchandise • Compound nouns	• *who* and *that* as the subject of a dependent clause • *that* as the object of a dependent clause
Unit 8 **Work** pages 96–107 Topic: **Success at work**	• Giving advice • Making suggestions • Explaining job responsibilities • Describing the duration of an activity	• Discussing work schedules • Talking about workplace problems and their solutions • Asking questions about work experiences	• Job responsibilities and skills • Prefixes and roots	• Contrasting present perfect and present perfect continuous • Adjectives ending in *-ed* and *-ing*
Review: Units 7 and 8 pages 108–109		• Understanding a class lecture		
Unit 9 **Daily living** pages 110–121 Topic: **Living green**	• Describing environmental issues and concerns • Giving advice • Making suggestions • Describing actions one can take	• Asking questions about "living green" • Discussing causes and effects of environmental problems • Discussing actions that could help the environment	• The environment • Synonyms	• Present unreal conditional • *since, due to, consequently, as a result*
Unit 10 **Leisure** pages 122–133 Topic: **Celebrations**	• Describing future possibility • Describing actions based on expectations • Expressing hopes and wishes • Comparing customs and celebrations	• Asking about and comparing wedding customs • Discussing possible and hypothetical holiday plans • Talking about hopes and wishes	• Celebrations • Words with multiple meanings	• Real future conditional and unreal conditional • *hope* and *wish*
Review: Units 9 and 10 pages 134–135		• Understanding a street interview		

Projects pages 136–140
Self-assessments pages 141–145
Reference pages 146–153
Irregular verbs page 154
Self-study audio script pages 155–161

READING	WRITING	LIFE SKILLS	PRONUNCIATION
• Reading a blog about videoconferencing • Recognizing the difference between facts and opinions	• Writing an expository paragraph about a time-saving device or activity • Using advantages and disadvantages to organize a paragraph	• Using a dictionary • Reading and understanding a table • Discussing Internet use • Discussing survey results	• Pronouncing key vocabulary
			• Stressed and unstressed words
• Reading a newspaper advice column about return policies • Recognizing synonyms	• Writing a persuasive paragraph about shopping online • Using transition words such as *first, second, next, furthermore, moreover,* and *finally* to signal a list of reasons in a paragraph	• Reading and understanding a returned-merchandise form • Talking about returning or exchanging merchandise	• Pronouncing key vocabulary
• Reading an article about hard and soft job skills • Reading a cover letter to apply for a job • Recognizing that quotations can explain or support a main idea	• Writing a cover letter to apply for a job • Including critical information in a cover letter	• Using a dictionary • Discussing a good work ethic • Reading and understanding a table about the fastest-growing service occupations • Discussing work skills	• Pronouncing key vocabulary
			• Stressing function words
• Reading a fable about how all things in life are connected • Asking questions to identify a cause-and-effect relationship	• Writing a paragraph about an environmental problem • Using cause and effect to organize a paragraph	• Using a dictionary or thesaurus • Reading and understanding a chart about reasons to "live green" • Discussing ways to help the environment	• Pronouncing key vocabulary
• Reading an article about special birthday celebrations around the world • Using punctuation as a clue to meaning	• Writing a descriptive paragraph about a favorite holiday or celebration • Concluding a paragraph by relating it to your personal life	• Using a dictionary • Reading and understanding a recipe • Discussing traditional meals and recipes	• Pronouncing key vocabulary
			• Identifying thought groups

To the teacher

What is *Ventures*?

Ventures is a five-level, standards-based, integrated-skills series for adult students. The five levels, which are Basic through Level Four, are for low-beginning literacy to high-intermediate students.

The *Ventures* series is flexible enough to be used in open enrollment, managed enrollment, and traditional programs. Its multilevel features support teachers who work with multilevel classes.

What components does *Ventures* have?

Student's Book with Self-study Audio CD

Each **Student's Book** contains a Welcome Unit and ten topic-focused units, plus five review units, one after every two units. Each unit has six skill-focused lessons. Projects, self-assessments, and a reference section are included at the back of the Student's Book.

- **Lessons** are self-contained, allowing for completion within a one-hour class period.
- **Review lessons** recycle, reinforce, and consolidate the materials presented in the previous two units and include a pronunciation activity.
- **Projects** offer community-building opportunities for students to work together – using the Internet or completing a task, such as making a poster or a book.
- **Self-assessments** are an important part of students' learning and success. They give students an opportunity to evaluate and reflect on their learning as well as a tool to support learner persistence.
- The **Self-study Audio CD** is included at the back of the Student's Book. The material on the CD is indicated in the Student's Book by an icon SELF-STUDY AUDIO CD .

Teacher's Edition with Teacher's Toolkit Audio CD/CD-ROM

The interleaved **Teacher's Edition** walks instructors step-by-step through the stages of a lesson.

- Included are learner-persistence and community-building tasks as well as teaching tips, expansion activities, and ways to expand a lesson to two or three instructional hours.

- The Student's Book answer key is included on the interleaved pages in the Teacher's Edition.
- The Teacher's Toolkit Audio CD/CD-ROM contains additional reproducible material for teacher support. Included are picture dictionary cards and worksheets (Levels 1 and 2), extended reading worksheets (Levels 3 and 4), tests with audio, and student self-assessments for portfolio assessment. Reproducible sheets also include cooperative learning activities. These activities reinforce the materials presented in the Student's Book and develop social skills, including those identified by SCANS[1] as being highly valued by employers.
- The unit, midterm, and final tests are found on both the Teacher's Toolkit Audio CD/CD-ROM and in the Teacher's Edition. The tests include listening, grammar, reading, and writing sections.

Audio Program

The *Ventures* series includes a **Class Audio** and a **Student Self-study Audio** SELF-STUDY AUDIO CD . The Class Audio contains all the listening materials in the Student's Book and is available on CD or audiocassette. The Student Self-study Audio CD contains all the unit conversations and readings from the Student's Book.

Workbook

The **Workbook** has two pages of activities for each lesson in the Student's Book.

- The exercises are designed so learners can complete them in class or independently. Students can check their own answers with the answer key in the back of the Workbook. Workbook exercises can be assigned in class, for homework, or as student support when a class is missed.
- Grammar charts and explanations at the back of the Workbook allow students to use the Workbook for self-study.
- If used in class, the Workbook can extend classroom instructional time by 30 minutes per lesson.

Add Ventures

Add Ventures is a book of reproducible worksheets designed for use in multilevel classrooms. The worksheets give students 15–30 minutes of additional practice with each lesson and can be used with

---

[1] The Secretary's Commission on Achieving Necessary Skills, which produced a document that identifies skills for success in the workplace. For more information, see wdr.doleta.gov/SCANS.

homogeneous or heterogeneous groupings. These worksheets can also be used as targeted homework practice at the level of individual students, ensuring learner success.

There are three tiered worksheets for each lesson.

- **Tier 1 Worksheets** provide additional practice for those who are at a level slightly below the Student's Book or who require more controlled practice.
- **Tier 2 Worksheets** provide additional practice for those who are on the level of the Student's Book.
- **Tier 3 Worksheets** provide additional practice that gradually expands beyond the Student's Book.

These multilevel worksheets are all keyed to the same answers for ease of classroom management.

Unit organization

Within each unit there are six lessons:

LESSON A Get ready The opening lesson focuses students on the topic of the unit. The initial exercise, *Talk about the pictures*, involves several pictures. The visuals create student interest in the topic and activate prior knowledge. They help the teacher assess what learners already know and serve as a prompt for the key vocabulary of each unit. Next is *Listening*, which is based on an extended conversation or several short conversations. The accompanying exercises give learners the opportunity to relate the spoken and written forms of new theme-related vocabulary. The lesson concludes with an opportunity for students to practice language related to the theme in a communicative activity.

LESSONS B and C focus on grammar. The sections move from a *Grammar focus* that presents the grammar point in chart form; to *Practice* exercises that check comprehension of the grammar point and provide guided practice; and, finally, to *Communicate* exercises that guide learners as they generate original answers and conversations. The sections on these pages are sometimes accompanied by a *Useful language* note, which provides explanations or expressions that can be used interchangeably to accomplish a specific language function.

LESSON D Reading develops reading skills and expands vocabulary. The lesson opens with a *Before you read* exercise, whose purpose is to activate prior knowledge and encourage learners to make predictions. A *Reading tip*, which focuses learners

on a specific reading skill, accompanies the *Read* exercise. The reading section of the lesson concludes with *After you read* exercises that check students' understanding. In the Basic Student's Book and Student's Books 1 and 2, the vocabulary expansion portion of the lesson is a *Picture dictionary*. It includes a *Word bank*, pictures to identify, and a conversation for practicing the new words. The words are intended to expand vocabulary related to the unit topic. In Student's Books 3 and 4, the vocabulary expansion portion of the lesson occurs in the *After you read* exercises. These exercises build awareness of word families, connotations, compound words, parts of speech, and other vocabulary expansion activities.

LESSON E Writing provides writing practice within the context of the unit. There are three kinds of exercises in the lesson: prewriting, writing, and postwriting. *Before you write* exercises provide warm-up activities to activate the language students will need for the writing and one or more exercises that provide a model for students to follow when they write. The *Write* exercise sets goals for the student writing. A *Writing tip*, which presents information about punctuation or organization directly related to the writing assignment, accompanies the *Write* exercise. In the *After you write* exercise, students share with a partner using guided questions and practice an important step in the writing process.

LESSON F Another view has three sections.

- **Life-skills reading** develops the scanning and skimming skills that are used with documents such as forms, charts, schedules, announcements, and ads. Multiple-choice questions that follow the document develop test-taking skills similar to CASAS[2] and BEST.[3] This section concludes with an exercise that encourages student communication by providing questions that focus on some aspect of information in the document.
- **Fun with language** provides exercises that review and sometimes expand the topic, vocabulary, or grammar of the unit. They are interactive activities for partner or group work.
- **Wrap up** refers students to the self-assessment page in the back of the book, where they can check their knowledge and evaluate their progress.

The Author Team

Gretchen Bitterlin   Sylvia Ramirez
Dennis Johnson   K. Lynn Savage
Donna Price

---

[2] The Comprehensive Adult Student Assessment System. For more information, see www.casas.org.
[3] The Basic English Skills Test. For more information, see www.cal.org/BEST.

Correlations

UNIT/PAGES	CASAS	EFF
Unit 1 **Personal information** pages 6–17	0.1.2, 0.1.4, 0.1.5, 0.1.6, 0.2.1, 0.2.4, 4.1.7, 4.1.8, 4.4.2, 4.5.2, 4.5.5, 4.6.1, 4.7.3, 4.8.1, 4.8.2, 7.1.1, 7.1.4, 7.2.3, 7.2.4, 7.4.1, 7.4.2, 7.4.5, 7.4.9, 7.5.1	Most EFF standards are met, with particular focus on: • Conveying ideas in writing • Cooperating with others • Listening actively • Reading with understanding • Speaking so others can understand • Taking responsibility for learning
Unit 2 **At school** pages 18–29	0.1.2, 0.1.5, 0.1.6, 0.2.1, 0.2.4, 2.3.1, 2.3.2, 2.5.5, 2.7.6, 4.1.4, 4.1.7, 4.1.9, 4.4.1, 4.6.1, 4.8.1, 4.8.2, 4.9.1, 6.0.1, 7.1.1, 7.1.4, 7.2.1, 7.2.2, 7.4.1, 7.4.2, 7.4.5, 7.5.1	Most EFF standards are met, with particular focus on: • Attending to oral information • Paying attention to the conventions of spoken English • Reflecting and evaluating • Selecting appropriate reading strategies • Speaking so others can understand • Understanding and working with pictures
Unit 3 **Friends and family** pages 32–43	0.1.2, 0.1.3, 0.1.4, 0.1.5, 0.2.2, 0.2.4, 4.4.3, 4.8.1, 4.8.2, 6.0.1, 6.6.5, 7.1.1, 7.1.4, 7.2.1, 7.2.3, 7.5.1, 7.5.5, 7.5.6, 8.3.1, 8.3.2	Most EFF standards are met, with particular focus on: • Conveying ideas in writing • Listening actively • Paying attention to the conventions of spoken English • Reading with understanding • Resolving conflict and negotiating • Taking responsibility for learning
Unit 4 **Health** pages 44–55	0.1.2, 0.1.3, 0.1.5, 0.2.4, 3.1.1, 3.5.2, 3.5.8, 3.5.9, 4.5.2, 4.5.5, 4.8.1, 6.0.1, 7.1.4, 7.2.1, 7.3.1, 7.3.2, 7.4.1, 7.4.2, 7.5.1, 7.5.5, 7.5.7, 8.3.1, 8.3.2	Most EFF standards are met, with particular focus on: • Advocating and influencing • Attending to oral information • Cooperating with others • Reading with understanding • Solving problems and making decisions • Speaking so others can understand
Unit 5 **Around town** pages 58–69	0.1.2, 0.1.5, 0.1.6, 0.2.4, 2.7.3, 3.1.3, 3.5.8, 3.5.9, 4.1.4, 4.8.1, 6.0.1, 7.1.1, 7.1.3, 7.1.4, 7.2.1, 7.2.2, 7.4.1, 7.4.2, 7.4.3, 7.5.1, 7.5.2, 7.5.5, 8.3.1, 8.3.2	Most EFF standards are met, with particular focus on: • Listening actively • Monitoring progress toward goals • Reading with understanding • Seeking feedback and revising accordingly • Speaking so others can understand • Understanding and working with pictures

SCANS	BEST Plus Form A	BEST Form B
Most SCANS standards are met, with particular focus on: • Demonstrating individual responsibility • Improving basic skills • Interpreting and communicating information • Knowing how to learn • Reasoning	Overall test preparation is supported, with particular impact on the following items: Locator: W5–6 Level 1: 4.2 Level 2: 4.2 Level 3: 4.1	Overall test preparation is supported, with particular impact on the following areas: • Employment • Oral interview • Personal information • Reading passages • Writing notes
Most SCANS standards are met, with particular focus on: • Acquiring and evaluating information • Participating as a member of a team • Serving clients and customers • Teaching others • Understanding systems	Overall test preparation is supported, with particular impact on the following items: Locator: W5 Level 3: 2.3	Overall test preparation is supported, with particular impact on the following areas: • Employment/Training • Oral interview • Personal information • Reading passages • Reading signs, ads, and notices • Time/Numbers • Writing notes
Most SCANS standards are met, with particular focus on: • Knowing how to learn • Negotiating • Organizing and maintaining information • Participating as a member of a team • Seeing things in the mind's eye	Overall test preparation is supported, with particular impact on the following items: Locator: W3 Level 2: 4.2 Level 3: 1.3, 2.3, 5.2	Overall test preparation is supported, with particular impact on the following areas: • Emergencies and safety • Housing • Oral interview • Personal information • Reading passages • Reading signs, ads, and notices • Time/Numbers • Writing notes
Most SCANS standards are met, with particular focus on: • Demonstrating individual responsibility and self-management • Improving basic skills • Making decisions • Reasoning • Solving problems	Overall test preparation is supported, with particular impact on the following items: Locator: W6 Level 3: 1, 1.2	Overall test preparation is supported, with particular impact on the following areas: • Health • Numbers • Oral interview • Personal information • Reading passages • Reading signs, ads, and notices • Shopping for food • Writing notes
Most SCANS standards are met, with particular focus on: • Demonstrating integrity • Interpreting and communicating information • Knowing how to learn • Organizing and maintaining information • Teaching others	Overall test preparation is supported, with particular impact on the following items: Locator: W5 Level 1: 4, 4.1, 4.2 Level 3: 2.2, 4, 4.1, 4.2	Overall test preparation is supported, with particular impact on the following areas: • Employment/Training • Oral interview • Personal information • Reading passages • Reading signs, ads, and notices • Time/Numbers • Writing notes

UNIT/PAGES	CASAS	EFF
Unit 6 **Time** pages 70–81	0.1.2, 0.1.5, 0.1.6, 0.2.4, 1.1.3, 1.3.1, 1.4.1, 1.7.4, 2.1.1, 2.2.3, 4.5.1, 4.5.2, 4.5.5, 4.8.1, 6.0.1, 7.1.1, 7.1.4, 7.2.1, 7.2.3, 7.2.4, 7.2.5, 7.4.1, 7.4.2, 7.4.8, 7.5.1	Most EFF standards are met, with particular focus on: • Conveying ideas in writing • Cooperating with others • Listening actively • Reading with understanding • Speaking so others can understand • Using information and communications technology
Unit 7 **Shopping** pages 84–95	0.1.2, 0.1.3, 0.1.5, 0.1.6, 1.2.2, 1.3.1, 1.3.3, 1.4.1, 1.6.3, 1.7.1, 4.8.1, 6.0.1, 7.1.1, 7.1.4, 7.2.1, 7.2.3, 7.2.5, 7.4.2, 7.4.3, 7.4.8, 7.5.1	Most EFF standards are met, with particular focus on: • Advocating and influencing • Attending to oral information • Reflecting and evaluating • Selecting appropriate reading strategies • Solving problems and making decisions • Taking responsibility for learning
Unit 8 **Work** pages 96–107	0.1.2, 0.1.3, 0.1.5, 0.2.4, 2.3.1, 2.3.2, 2.4.1, 4.1.2, 4.1.6, 4.1.7, 4.1.8, 4.4.1, 4.4.2, 4.4.3, 4.4.4, 4.5.2, 4.5.5, 4.6.2, 4.7.3, 4.8.1, 4.8.2, 6.0.1, 7.1.1, 7.1.4, 7.2.1, 7.2.3, 7.2.7, 7.3.1, 7.3.2, 7.4.1, 7.4.2, 7.4.5, 7.5.1, 7.5.2, 7.5.6	Most EFF standards are met, with particular focus on: • Attending to oral information • Monitoring comprehension and adjusting reading strategies • Paying attention to the conventions of spoken English • Seeking input from others • Taking stock of where one is • Understanding and working with pictures
Unit 9 **Daily living** pages 110–121	0.1.2, 0.1.5, 1.4.1, 2.2.3, 2.3.3, 2.7.3, 4.8.1, 5.6.1, 5.7.1, 7.1.1, 7.2.1, 7.2.2, 7.2.6, 7.3.1, 7.3.2, 7.3.4, 7.4.2, 7.4.3, 7.5.1, 7.5.4, 8.3.1	Most EFF standards are met, with particular focus on: • Conveying ideas in writing • Guiding others • Listening actively • Reading with understanding • Solving problems and making decisions • Speaking so others can understand
Unit 10 **Leisure** pages 122–133	0.1.1, 0.1.2, 0.1.5, 0.1.6, 0.2.4, 1.1.1, 1.1.5, 2.3.2, 2.5.7, 2.7.1, 2.7.2, 2.7.4, 4.5.2, 4.5.5, 4.8.1, 6.0.1, 7.1.1, 7.1.4, 7.2.1, 7.2.3, 7.2.4, 7.2.6, 7.4.1, 7.4.2, 7.4.4, 7.4.5, 7.5.1, 7.5.6	Most EFF standards are met, with particular focus on: • Attending to oral information • Attending to visual sources of information • Interacting with others in positive ways • Paying attention to the conventions of written English • Reading with understanding • Selecting appropriate reading strategies

SCANS	BEST Plus Form A	BEST Form B
Most SCANS standards are met, with particular focus on: • Applying technology to task • Improving basic skills • Interpreting and communicating information • Knowing how to learn • Selecting technology	Overall test preparation is supported, with particular impact on the following items: Locator: W5 Level 2: 2.3	Overall test preparation is supported, with particular impact on the following areas: • Oral interview • Personal information • Reading passages • Numbers • Writing notes
Most SCANS standards are met, with particular focus on: • Demonstrating individual responsibility and self-management • Organizing and maintaining information • Seeing things in the mind's eye • Solving problems • Understanding systems	Overall test preparation is supported, with particular impact on the following items: Level 1: 1.2, 1.3 Level 2: 3.1, 3.2, 3.3	Overall test preparation is supported, with particular impact on the following areas: • Numbers • Oral interview • Personal information • Reading passages • Reading signs, ads, and notices • Shopping
Most SCANS standards are met, with particular focus on: • Acquiring and evaluating information • Allocating human resources • Knowing how to learn • Participating as a member of a team • Reasoning	Overall test preparation is supported, with particular impact on the following items: Locator: W5 Level 3: 2.3	Overall test preparation is supported, with particular impact on the following areas: • Employment/Training • Envelopes • Oral interview • Personal information • Reading passages • Time/Numbers • Writing notes
Most SCANS standards are met, with particular focus on: • Improving basic skills • Knowing how to learn • Seeing things in the mind's eye • Teaching others • Understanding systems	Overall test preparation is supported, with particular impact on the following items: Level 1: 2.3, 3.2, 3.3 Level 2: 2.1, 2.2, 2.3 Level 3: 3.3	Overall test preparation is supported, with particular impact on the following areas: • Emergencies/Housing • Reading signs, ads, and notices • Safety • Oral interview • Personal information • Reading passages • Writing notes
Most SCANS standards are met, with particular focus on: • Applying technology to task • Improving basic skills • Organizing and maintaining information • Thinking creatively • Working with cultural diversity	Overall test preparation is supported, with particular impact on the following items: Locator: W1, W7 Level 1: 4.2 Level 3: 4.1	Overall test preparation is supported, with particular impact on the following areas: • Calendar • Food labels • Numbers • Oral interview • Personal information • Reading passages • Shopping • Writing notes

Meet the Ventures author team

Gretchen Bitterlin has been an ESL instructor and ESL department instructional leader with the Continuing Education Program, San Diego Community College District. She now coordinates that agency's large noncredit ESL program. She was also an ESL Teacher Institute Trainer and Chair of the TESOL Task Force on Adult Education Program Standards. She is a co-author of *English for Adult Competency*.

Dennis Johnson has been an ESL instructor at City College of San Francisco, teaching all levels of ESL, since 1977. As ESL Site Coordinator, he has provided guidance to faculty in selecting textbooks. He is the author of *Get Up and Go* and co-author of *The Immigrant Experience*.

Donna Price is Associate Professor of ESL and Vocational ESL/Technology Resource Instructor for the Continuing Education Program, San Diego Community College District. She has taught all levels of ESL for 20 years and is a former recipient of the TESOL Newbury House Award for Excellence in Teaching. She is also the author of *Skills for Success*.

Sylvia Ramirez is a professor at MiraCosta College, where she coordinates the large noncredit ESL program. She has more than 30 years of experience in adult ESL, including multilevel ESL, vocational ESL, family literacy, and distance learning. She has represented the California State Department of Education in providing technical assistance to local ESL programs.

K. Lynn Savage, Series Editor, is a retired ESL teacher and Vocational ESL Resource teacher from City College of San Francisco, who trains teachers for adult education programs around the country. She chaired the committee that developed *ESL Model Standards for Adult Education Programs* (California, 1992) and is the author, co-author, and editor of many ESL materials including *Teacher Training through Video*, *Parenting for Academic Success: A Curriculum for Families Learning English*, *Crossroads Café*, *Building Life Skills*, *Picture Stories*, *May I Help You?*, and *English That Works*.

To the student

Welcome to *Ventures 4*! We want you to enjoy using your *Ventures* Student's Book in your classroom. We also hope that you will use this book to study on your own. For that reason, the Student's Book comes with an audio CD. Use it at home to review and practice the material you are learning in class. You will make faster progress in learning English if you take the time to study at home and do your homework.

Good luck in your studies!

The Author Team
Gretchen Bitterlin
Dennis Johnson
Donna Price
Sylvia Ramirez
K. Lynn Savage

Welcome

1 Meet your classmates

A Look at the picture. What do you see?

B What are the people doing?

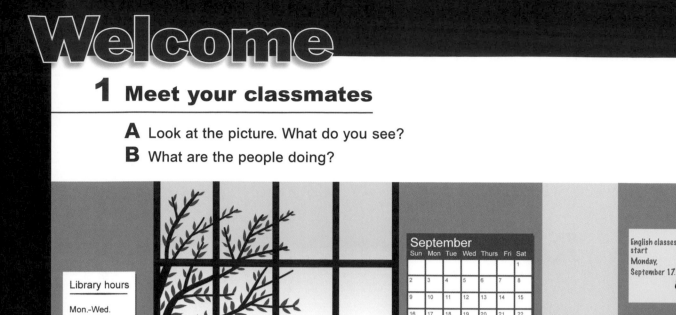

Library hours

Mon.-Wed.
9 a.m.-9 p.m.
Thurs.-Sat.
9 a.m.-6 p.m.

September

Sun	Mon	Tue	Wed	Thurs	Fri	Sat
						1
2	3	4	5	6	7	8
9	10	11	12	13	14	15
16	17	18	19	20	21	22
23	24	25	26	27	28	29
30						

Return books here.

English classes start Monday, September 17.

C-D

A-B

2 Introductions: What kind of person are you?

A **Read** the list of adjectives. Add two more. Put a check (✓) next to the ones that describe you.

☐ active	☐ confident	☐ intelligent	☐ quiet
☐ artistic	☐ creative	☐ kind	☐ reliable
☐ busy	☐ enthusiastic	☐ nice	☐ shy
☐ careful	☐ friendly	☐ outgoing	☐ strong
☐ caring	☐ fun-loving	☐ patient	☐ _____
☐ clever	☐ honest	☐ punctual	☐ _____

B **Read** the list of activities. Add two more. Put a check (✓) next to the ones you enjoy doing.

☐ camping	☐ reading	☐ using the Internet
☐ cleaning the house	☐ shopping	☐ volunteering
☐ cooking	☐ singing	☐ washing dishes
☐ dancing	☐ socializing	☐ watching TV
☐ helping people	☐ staying home	☐ working out
☐ painting	☐ talking on the phone	☐ _____
☐ playing sports	☐ traveling	☐ _____

C **Talk** with a partner. Ask questions. Write your partner's answers.

1. What are some adjectives that describe you?

_____

2. What are some activities that you enjoy doing?

_____

3. What are some activities that you dislike?

_____

D **Write** sentences about your partner.

My partner's name: _____

1. My partner is _____ .

2. My partner enjoys _____ .

3. My partner dislikes _____ .

E **Introduce** your partner to the class.

3 Verb tense review

SELF-STUDY AUDIO CD

A 🔊 **Listen** to each sentence. Circle the verb form you hear.

1. (cleans)   cleaned
2. lived   has lived
3. was talking   talked
4. is looking   is going to look

5. has been making   is making
6. has been working is working
7. was watching   is watching
8. were waiting   have been waiting

SELF-STUDY AUDIO CD

🔊 **Listen again.** Check your answers.

B **Read.** Complete the story. Use the correct verb form.

Last Monday evening, I _was driving_ home from work when
                              1. drive

I _____ a car accident. It _____ dark,
        2. have   3. be

and it _____ . About five blocks from my house, I
           4. rain

_____ for a red light. While I _____ for
    5. stop   6. wait

the light to change, another car _____ my car. I guess
                                      7. hit

the driver _____ me because of the rain. The accident
              8. not / see

_____ my car badly.
    9. damage

    Since the accident, I _____ to work by bus. It's
                              10. go

really inconvenient because I _____ more than 20
                                  11. work

miles from my home. The bus is slow, and I _____
                                                12. be

late several times already. It _____ at least two more
                                  13. take

weeks to fix my car. Until then, I _____ to find a
                                        14. need

better way to get to work. I _____ to be late anymore.
                                15. not / want

SELF-STUDY AUDIO CD

🔊 **Listen** and check your answers.

C **Talk** in a small group. Ask and answer the questions.

1. Have you ever had or seen a car accident?
2. What were you doing before the accident happened?
3. Describe the accident. Explain what happened.

4   Welcome

4 Study habits and strategies

A Talk with a partner about study habits and strategies for learning English. Ask questions. Check (✓) your partner's answers.

Partner's name: _____ Have you ever . . . ?	Yes, I have.	No, I haven't.
made vocabulary cards		
used a dictionary to learn new words		
asked a stranger a question in English		
studied English with a friend		
used a to-do list to organize your time		
tried to guess the meaning of new words		

Talk with a different partner. Tell about the classmate you interviewed.

> Carmen has made vocabulary cards. She hasn't used a to-do list.

B Talk with your classmates. Complete the chart.

> Song Mi, do you watch TV in English every day?

> Yes, I do.

Find a classmate who . . .	Name
1. watches TV in English every day	Song Mi *del* *yes, I dotote*
2. asks questions when he or she doesn't understand	*yes*
3. underlines important information in textbooks	
4. likes to sing songs in English	*yes, I do*
5. speaks English at work	
6. sets goals for learning	
7. writes new English words in a notebook	*yes, I do*
8. reads newspapers and magazines in English	*yes, I do*

Share information about your classmates.

> Song Mi watches TV in English every day.

Lesson A *Get ready*

1 Talk about the pictures

A What do you see?

B What is happening?

2 Listening

SELF-STUDY
AUDIO CD **A** 🔊 **Listen** and answer the questions.

1. Who are the speakers?
2. What are they talking about?

SELF-STUDY
AUDIO CD **B** 🔊 **Listen again.** Complete the chart.

Family member	Good at	Example
1. Brenda	*math*	*got first place in a math contest*
2. Gerry		
3. Danny		
4. Nina		

Listen again. Check your answers.

SELF-STUDY
AUDIO CD **C** 🔊 **Read.** Complete the story. Listen and check your answers.

aptitude	bright	gifted in	mechanical
brain	fixing up	mathematical	musical

Emily stops by Nina's house on her way home from jogging. They talk about Nina's three children. Brenda is very _mathematical_ . She's just
1
won a math contest at school. When Emily calls Brenda a _____ ,
2
Nina says that all her children are _____ , but in different ways.
3
Gerry isn't _____ math, but he's very _____ . He plays
4   5
and sings very well and even writes music. Danny is the _____
6
one in the family. He's good at _____ old cars. Emily thinks
7
that Nina is also smart because she is such a good cook. Emily has no
_____ for cooking.
8

D **Discuss.** Talk with your classmates.

1. How are the three children different?
2. Do you think that one child is more intelligent than the others? Why or why not?
3. Do you think that Nina is a good parent? Why or why not?

Noun clauses

1 Grammar focus: noun clauses with *that*

Statements and questions

Emily realizes that Brenda has a good brain.
People say that Gerry plays the guitar very well.
Do you think that people are smart in different ways?
Do you feel that you're smart?

Introductory clauses

I think . . .	Do you think . . . ?
I feel . . .	Do you feel . . . ?
He realizes . . .	Does he realize . . . ?
People believe . . .	Do people believe . . . ?

For a grammar explanation, turn to page 146.

Useful language

When speaking, we frequently omit *that* before a noun clause.

People think **that** she's smart.
People think she's smart.

2 Practice

A Write. Write sentences with *that* and a noun clause.

1. There are many kinds of intelligence. (Do you believe . . . ?)
   Do you believe that there are many kinds of intelligence?

2. Nina has an interesting family. (Do you think . . . ?)
   _____

3. She is very gifted in math. (Brenda's teacher agrees . . .)
   _____

4. Gerry will be a famous musician someday. (Everyone believes . . .)
   _____

5. Danny has an aptitude for fixing up cars. (I didn't realize . . .)
   _____

6. Mechanical skills are very important. (Do you feel . . . ?)
   _____

7. Nina is good at cooking. (Do you think . . . ?)
   _____

Listen and check your answers.

B Talk with a partner. Look at the picture. Answer the questions. Use introductory clauses from the box.

| I believe . . . | I suppose . . . | I think . . . | I'd say . . . | I'm sure . . . |

> **A** I think (that) the young man is about 26.
> **B** I'd say (that) the young man is only 20.

1. How old are they?
2. Where are they going?
3. Where are they coming from?

4. What do they do for a living?
5. What are they good at?
6. What aren't they good at?

Write sentences about your opinions.

I think that the young man is about 26 years old.

3 Communicate

A Work in a small group. Give your opinions. Use *I believe, I think, I'd say, I don't believe,* and other introductory clauses.

1. Are women more talkative than men?
2. Are boys better at math and science than girls?
3. Are men more mechanical than women?
4. Are women more musical than men?
5. Are men more interested in sports than women?
6. Can women do the same jobs as men?

B Share your classmates' opinions.

> **Useful language**
> *I (totally) agree with you.*
> *I (strongly) disagree.*

> **Culture note**
> Studies have shown that girls and boys in the United States have a similar aptitude for math and science when they start elementary school.

Parts of speech

1 Grammar focus: contrasting adjectives and adverbs

Adjectives	Adverbs
Helen is an intelligent girl.	She talks very intelligently.
I am a slow driver.	I drive slowly.
You're a good dancer.	You dance well.
It was an easy game.	He won easily.

Irregular	
Adjectives	**Adverbs**
fast	fast
good	well
hard	hard

For a grammar explanation, turn to page 146.

For a grammar explanation, turn to page 146.

2 Practice

A Write. Complete the sentences with adjectives or adverbs.

1. Carol speaks very ___*intelligently*___ . She's a ___*bright*___ girl.
   (intelligent)   (bright)

2. That isn't a _____ guitar, but he's playing it _____ .
   (bad)   (bad)

3. Benny is an _____ cook. His dinner last night was _____ .
   (excellent)   (fantastic)

4. The mechanic did a _____ job on my car. Now it runs _____ .
   (good)   (perfect)

5. You danced very _____ in the dance contest. You were _____ !
   (skillful)   (wonderful)

6. I don't type very _____ . I can't move my fingers very _____ .
   (fast)   (quick)

7. That writing test was really _____ . Writing is not an _____
   (hard)   (easy)

   subject for me.

8. You sang that song _____ ! I didn't know you could sing
   (beautiful)

   so _____ !
   (good)

9. Your report is _____ . You wrote it very _____ .
   (great)   (clear)

10. I work _____ . I have to be very _____ .
    (slow)   (careful)

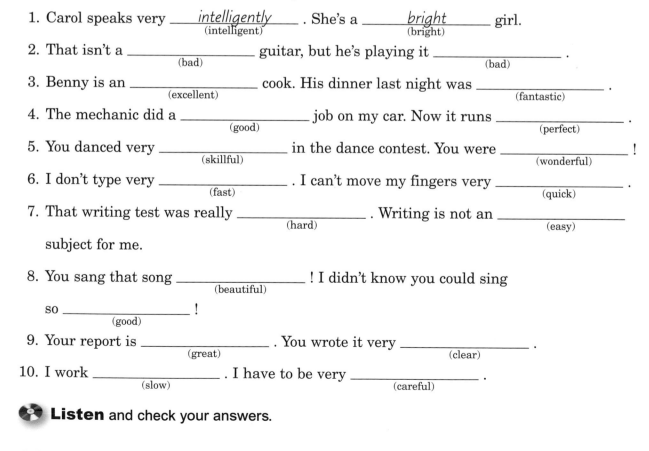 **Listen** and check your answers.

B **Talk** with a partner. Ask and answer questions about the pictures. Use the adjective or adverb form of the words in the box.

A What kind of artist is he?
B He's a skillful artist.

A How does he paint?
B He paints beautifully.

beautiful	excellent	good	skillful
careful	fast	professional	wonderful

artist / paint

seamstress / sew

driver / drive

carpenter / work

singer / sing

dancers / dance

Write sentences about the people.

He's a skillful artist. He paints beautifully.

3 Communicate

A **Work** in a small group. Ask and answer the questions.

1. What kind of student are you?
2. How do you speak English?
3. What can you do very well?
4. What is difficult for you?
5. What can you do perfectly?
6. What do you do very fast?

B **Share** information about your classmates.

Armando says he's an excellent student.

1 Before you read

Talk with a partner. Look at the reading tip. Answer the questions.

1. What is this article about?
2. How many ways are there to be smart, according to the article?

> Before you begin reading, skim — look at the title, headings, and boldfaced words — to get a general idea of what the reading is about.

2 Read

SELF-STUDY AUDIO CD **Read** the magazine article. Listen and read again.

Many Ways to Be Smart

Josh is a star on the school baseball team. He gets Ds and Fs on all his math tests. His brother Frank can't catch, throw, or hit a baseball, but he easily gets As in math. Which boy do you think is more intelligent? Howard Gardner, a professor of education at Harvard University, would say that Josh and Frank are both smart, but in different ways. His theory of multiple intelligences identifies eight different "intelligences" to explain the way people understand, experience, and learn about the world around them.

Verbal / Linguistic
Some people are good with words. They prefer to learn by reading, listening, and speaking.

Bodily / Kinesthetic
Some people are "body smart." They are often athletic. Kinesthetic learners learn best when they are moving.

Logical / Mathematical
These people have an aptitude for math. They like solving logic problems and puzzles.

Interpersonal
Certain people are "group smart." They easily understand other people. They are good at communicating and interacting with others.

Musical / Rhythmical
These people are sensitive to sound, melodies, and rhythms. They are gifted in singing, playing instruments, or composing music.

Intrapersonal
Some people are "self smart." They can understand their own feelings and emotions. They often enjoy spending time alone.

Visual / Spatial
These "picture people" are often good at drawing or painting. They are sensitive to colors and designs.

Naturalist
These people are skilled in working with plants and animals in the natural world.

According to Gardner, many people have several or even all of these intelligences, but most of us have one or two intelligences that are primary, or strongest.

3 After you read

A Check your understanding.

Which primary intelligence do these people have?

1. Josh Dillon, age 16: A star on the school baseball team; loves all sports; plans to become a coach.	*bodily / kinesthetic*
2. Ida Grove, age 45: Knows the name of everything in her garden.	
3. Manisha Pari, age 22: Writes in her journal every day about her feelings; enjoys taking walks by herself.	
4. Joy Rhee, age 30: Writes short stories and enjoys poetry.	
5. Susana Ochoa, age 42: Vocational counselor at a community college; volunteers at her church every Sunday.	
6. Amal Mohammed, age 27: Photographer; takes art classes.	

B Build your vocabulary.

Understanding prefixes and roots of words will help you learn new words.

1. Find an example in the reading of each prefix or root. Write it in the chart.

2. Use a dictionary. Write the meaning of the words.

3. Guess the meaning of the prefixes and roots in the chart.

	Example from reading	Meaning of word	Meaning of prefix or root
Prefixes			
1. *intra-*	*intrapersonal*	*inside a person's mind or self*	*in, inside*
2. *inter-*			
3. *multi-*			
Roots			
4. *kine*			
5. *log*			
6. *prim*			
7. *vis*			

C Talk with a partner.

1. What is your primary intelligence?
2. What are good jobs for people with the following intelligences: intrapersonal, interpersonal, kinesthetic, logical, and visual?

Writing

1 Before you write

A **Write** *1* through *4* next to your strongest intelligences. (Your primary intelligence should be number 1.) Compare with your classmates.

_____ Verbal / Linguistic   _____ Bodily / Kinesthetic
_____ Logical / Mathematical   _____ Interpersonal
_____ Musical / Rhythmical   _____ Intrapersonal
_____ Visual / Spatial   _____ Naturalist

B **Read** the writing tip. Then read the model paragraphs. Choose the best topic sentence for each paragraph. Write it on the line.

> A good paragraph has a topic sentence and supporting sentences. The topic sentence tells what the paragraph is about.

1. **Topic sentence:**
   a. I enjoy taking my flute to the park.
   b. My primary intelligence is musical.

   _____ All my life, I've enjoyed singing and playing the flute. While I was growing up, my favorite classes were always music classes. I've taken private music lessons and also attended special summer music camps. I think that I can play well, and I also like to write original songs. On weekends, I enjoy taking my flute to a nearby park. There, I sit on the grass and play my music for hours. If I'm not playing, I'm listening to the music of the birds and the wind in the trees.

2. **Topic sentence:**
   a. My strongest intelligence is mathematical.
   b. In school, my favorite subject was mathematics.

   _____ My parents say that I started counting before I was two years old. I've always liked to play games with numbers. I never forget my friends' birthdays or telephone numbers. I like to keep track of my monthly expenses so that I stay within my budget. Other people complain that balancing their checkbooks is hard, but I enjoy it. My aptitude for mathematics helps me in every part of my life.

C Complete the outline.

Read these supporting details about a person with kinesthetic intelligence.
Write a topic sentence.

Topic sentence: _____

Supporting details:
- Since I was a child, I have loved to move my body.
- I've taken many types of dance classes, including ballet, modern, jazz, swing, salsa, and African.
- I can dance to any kind of music that I hear.
- My friends say that I'm a great dancer.

D Plan a paragraph about your primary intelligence. Use the outline to make notes on your ideas.

Topic sentence: _____

Supporting details:

- _____
- _____
- _____
- _____
- _____

2 Write

Write a paragraph about your primary intelligence. Use the paragraphs in Exercise 1B and the outlines in Exercises 1C and 1D to help you.

3 After you write

A Check your writing.

	Yes	No
1. I started my paragraph with a general topic sentence.	☐	☐
2. I gave specific details to support my topic sentence.	☐	☐
3. I used noun clauses, adjectives, and adverbs correctly.	☐	☐

B Share your writing with a partner.

1. Take turns. Read your paragraph to a partner.
2. Comment on your partner's paragraph. Ask your partner a question about the paragraph. Tell your partner one thing you learned.

Lesson F *Another view*

1 Life-skills reading

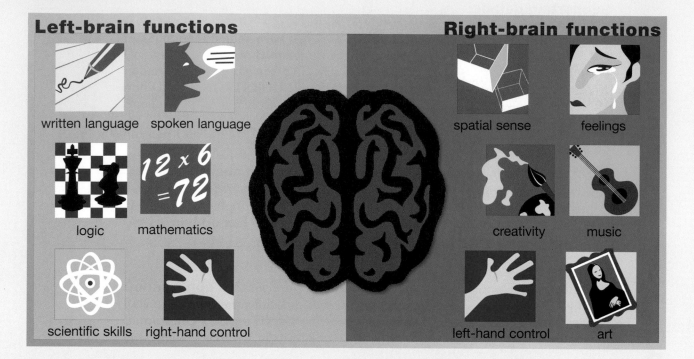

Left-brain functions

written language   spoken language

logic   mathematics

scientific skills   right-hand control

Right-brain functions

spatial sense   feelings

creativity   music

left-hand control   art

A Read the questions. Look at the diagram. Circle the answers.

1. Which side of the brain controls verbal ability?
   a. left side
   b. right side
   c. both sides
   d. none of the above

2. Which abilities are right-brain functions?
   a. art
   b. music
   c. creativity
   d. all of the above

3. Which ability is a left-brain function?
   a. spatial sense
   b. logic
   c. feelings
   d. none of the above

4. Which sentence is true?
   a. The left brain controls the left hand.
   b. The right brain controls the right hand.
   c. The left brain controls the right hand.
   d. none of the above

5. What can you say about "left-brained" people?
   a. They go to sleep easily.
   b. They are very musical.
   c. They are artistic.
   d. They are logical.

6. Which intelligence is a right-brain intelligence?
   a. musical / rhythmical
   b. logical / mathematical
   c. linguistic
   d. a and b

B Talk with a partner. Are you a right-brained or a left-brained person? What about the other people in your family?

16   Unit 1

2 Fun with language

A **Work** in a small group. What are these people famous for?
What are their intelligences?

Bodily / Kinesthetic	Intrapersonal	Musical / Rhythmical	Verbal / Linguistic
Interpersonal	Logical / Mathematical	Naturalist	Visual / Spatial

1 Princess Diana

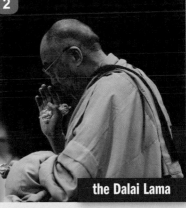
2 the Dalai Lama

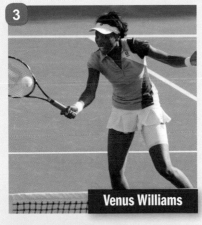
3 Venus Williams

4 Pablo Picasso

5 Christina Aguilera

6 Albert Einstein

Name some other famous people and describe their intelligences.

B **Talk** with your classmates. Which statements are true for you?
What kind of intelligence is related to each statement?

1. I'm an animal lover.
2. It's difficult for me to sit still for long.
3. I enjoy taking lots of photographs.
4. I'm very skillful with my hands.
5. I frequently play board games like chess or mah-jongg.
6. I like to go fishing.
7. I have many close friends.
8. I usually listen to music while I'm working or relaxing.
9. My checkbook is always balanced.
10. Other people think that I'm a good leader.

3 Wrap up

Complete the **Self-assessment** on page 141.

Get ready

1 Talk about the pictures

A What do you see?

B What is happening?

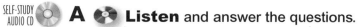
2 Listening

SELF-STUDY
AUDIO CD

A **Listen** and answer the questions.

1. Who are the speakers?
2. What are they talking about?

SELF-STUDY
AUDIO CD

B **Listen again.** Complete the chart.

1. Type of certificate	*Hospitality and Tourism*
2. Places of employment	
3. Number of required classes	
4. Time to complete the program	
5. Cost per unit	
6. Estimated cost to earn the certificate	

Listen again. Check your answers.

SELF-STUDY
AUDIO CD

C **Read.** Complete the story. Listen and check your answers.

bilingual	high-paying	internship	qualify
deadline	industry	motivated	requirements

Vasili hears a radio ad about the Hospitality and Tourism certificate program at La Costa Community College. The ad says graduates can find ___*high-paying*___ jobs in the tourism _____ . Vasili goes to see his
1   2
ESL counselor, Mrs. Ochoa. She tells him about the program _____ ,
3
which include an _____ in a local tourism business. She also tells
4
him about the _____ for registration, and she says there is financial
5
aid for students who _____ . Vasili is concerned about his English,
6
but Mrs. Ochoa tells him not to worry. Vasili is _____ , he's very
7
_____ , and he has good interpersonal skills.
8

D **Discuss.** Talk with your classmates. Is hospitality and tourism a good industry for Vasili? Would you like this type of career? Why or why not?

Lesson B *The passive voice*

1 Grammar focus: the present passive

Active	Passive
The college gives a placement test.	A placement test is given (by the college).
The college offers online classes every semester.	Online classes are offered (by the college) every semester.
Does the college offer financial aid?	Is financial aid offered (by the college)?
When does the college arrange internships?	When are internships arranged (by the college)?

For a grammar explanation, turn to page 147.
For a list of past participles, turn to page 154.

Useful language
You can leave out the "by" phrase if the "doer" of the action is unknown or unimportant.

2 Practice

A Write. Complete the sentences. Use the present passive voice.

1. **A** When ____*is*____ the English placement test ____*given*____ to
   new students?   (give)

   B The English placement test _____ a week before the
   first day of class.   (administer)

2. **A** _____ a math placement test also _____ ?
                                                      (require)
   B No, a math placement test _____ not _____ .
                                                           (need)

3. **A** Where _____ the financial aid office _____ ?
                                                         (locate)
   B It _____ next to the admissions office.
                   (locate)

4. **A** Where _____ the classes _____ ?
                                              (hold)
   B Most of the classes _____ in the business building.
                                      (hold)

5. **A** _____ classes _____ at different times?
                                  (offer)
   B Yes. Both day and evening classes _____ .
                                                      (offer)

6. **A** _____ job placement services _____ to graduates?
                                                  (provide)
   B Yes. Job help _____ to students who qualify.
                              (offer)

Listen and check your answers. Then practice with a partner.

B Talk with a partner. Read about two courses in the Hospitality and Tourism Certificate Program. Ask and answer questions using the present passive. Use the past participles in the box.

given	held	located	offered	required

A When is HOSP 100 offered?
B It's offered in the fall and spring.

A Are day and evening classes given?
B Yes, they are.

La Costa Community College Course Schedule
Hospitality and Tourism Certificate Program

HOSP 100: Introduction to Hospitality and Tourism
Requirement: Pass an English placement test.
Fall and spring
T / Th 10:00–11:30 a.m.
M / W 6:00–7:30 p.m.
Room: T130

BUS 137: Customer Service
Requirement: Pass HOSP 100.
Spring
T / Th 8:00–9:30 a.m.
(Online course also available.)
Room: B480

Write sentences about the courses.

HOSP 100 is offered in the fall and spring.

3 Communicate

A Work with a partner. Role-play a conversation between a counselor and a student who wants to enroll in the Auto Mechanics Certificate Program. Ask and answer questions about the topics.

- online courses
- required courses
- English or math placement tests
- location of classes
- internships
- financial aid
- job counseling

Student Are online courses offered in the Auto Mechanics Certificate Program?
Counselor No. Online courses are not offered in that program.
Student What about internships?
Counselor Internships are arranged for each student in the program.

B Perform your role play for the class.

Lesson C *The passive voice*

1 Grammar focus: infinitives after passive verbs

Students are told to arrive early on the first day of class.

Everyone is encouraged to attend class regularly.

Are students expected to do homework every night?

How often are students expected to meet with their counselors?

For a grammar explanation, turn to page 147.

For a list of common infinitives after passive verbs, turn to page 147.

2 Practice

A Write complete statements or questions. Use the present passive with infinitives.

1. applicants / expect / meet / all application deadlines.

   Applicants are expected to meet all application deadlines.

2. new students / tell / come early / for registration.

   _____

3. all new students / require / take / a writing test?

   _____

4. some students / advise / enroll / in an English composition class.

   _____

5. students / expect / attend / every class?

   _____

6. students / encourage / meet / with a counselor regularly.

   _____

7. when / participants / expect / complete / their internships?

   _____

8. students / require / earn / a grade of C or better in each course.

   _____

9. students / tell / study / with a partner and to go to tutoring often.

   _____

   Listen and check your answers.

B Talk with a partner. Read the ad. Make statements about the Work Experience Program. Use the past participles in the box.

| allowed | encouraged | expected | required | told |

> Students are allowed to earn college credit for work experience.

Work Experience Program at La Costa Community College

Earn college credit for the job you have.

You can earn up to 4 units of credit by participating in the program.

To enroll, attend an orientation session. Then work at least 75 paid hours or 60 volunteer hours. Questions?

Contact the Career Center at 777-555-2222, or visit our Web site.

www.lacosta.edu/workexperience

Write sentences about the Work Experience Program at La Costa Community College.

Students are allowed to earn college credit for work experience.

Culture note
Work experience programs exist in many U.S. colleges to help adult students get credit for past and present work experience.

3 Communicate

A Work with a partner. Ask and answer questions about the requirements at a school, course, or program that your partner knows. Discuss the items listed below.

- placement tests
- counselors
- dates and times of classes
- location
- registration fees
- attendance
- textbooks
- tutors
- homework

> *A* At high schools in your native country, are students given a placement test?
> *B* Yes. Every new student is required to take a placement test.

B Share information with your classmates.

1 Before you read

Talk with a partner. Look at the reading tip. Answer the questions.

1. Who is the story about?
2. What was one obstacle to their success?
3. What places are mentioned in the reading?

2 Read

SELF-STUDY
AUDIO CD

Read the newspaper article. Listen and read again.

> Scan a reading to find specific information such as names, places, and key words.

An Immigrant Family's Success Story

Choi and Lili Wei left China with their baby boy in the late 1980s. They were poor field workers in their native country, and they wanted their child to have the opportunities they lacked. They arrived in New York and found a one-bedroom apartment in a poor, unstable area. They could only afford a bicycle for transportation, yet they felt fortunate to have the chance to begin a new life in the United States.

Choi and Lili faced many obstacles because they couldn't speak English and had no skills. They found night work cleaning businesses and restaurants. They saved every penny, and after six years, they were able to buy a small restaurant of their own.

They were determined to learn English, get an education, and make a good life for their son. The couple sacrificed a great deal. They never went to a movie, never ate out, and hardly ever bought anything extra. In their free time, they attended English and citizenship classes. Both of them eventually earned their GED certificates. Choi then enrolled in college while Lili worked in the restaurant.

This past spring, Choi fulfilled a lifelong dream of graduating from college. Now he is registered in a master's degree program in business beginning this fall. And what about their "baby" boy? Their son, Peter, now 21, received a scholarship to a private university, where he is working on his own dream to become an architect.

Choi and Lili are proud to be models of the "American dream." Choi has this advice for other new immigrants: "Find your passion, make a plan to succeed, and don't ever give up."

3 After you read

A Check your understanding.

1. What was Choi and Lili's native country?
2. What kind of work did they do before they came to the United States?
3. Why did they decide to come to the United States?
4. What kind of job did they find in the United States?
5. What did Choi and Lili do when they weren't working?
6. What is Peter's dream?
7. What is Choi's advice for people who want to succeed?

B Build your vocabulary.

1. Find and underline the following words in the story: *lacked*, *unstable*, *fortunate*, *obstacles*, *determined*, and *passion*.

2. Find three more words that you do not know. Write them here:

   _____   _____   _____

3. Look up all the words in a dictionary. Make a vocabulary card for each word. On one side of the card, write the word and the part of speech. On the other side, write the definition and your own sentence using the word.

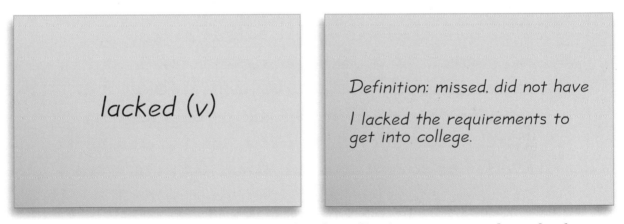

lacked (v)

Definition: missed. did not have

I lacked the requirements to get into college.

Abbreviations for parts of speech: v = verb; adj = adjective; n = noun; adv = adverb

C Talk with a partner.

1. Do you believe that you are fortunate? Why or why not?
2. What are you determined to do?
3. Have you found your passion? What is it?
4. What is one obstacle you have faced?

Writing

1 Before you write

A Talk with your classmates. Answer the questions.

1. Do you know a successful person?
2. Why is this person successful?
3. What did the person do to become successful?
4. What was one obstacle to this person's success?

B Read the paragraph.

> ### My Successful Cousin
>
> My cousin, Daniel, is the most successful person I know. However, he has had many obstacles on his road to success. First of all, his parents died in an automobile accident when he was 17 years old. Daniel needed to take care of his two younger brothers, so he quit school and found a job at a local supermarket. When his brothers were in school, he worked. At night, he helped them with homework and did all the chores. Even with all his responsibilities, Daniel was a very reliable worker. His boss decided to help him go to college. It took Daniel eight years, but finally he graduated. Now Daniel plans to enroll in a business management course. If he is accepted, he hopes to open his own business someday. Daniel has a dream, and he is working hard to achieve his dream. He is my hero!

Use specific details such as facts, examples, and reasons to support your topic sentence.

C Talk with a partner.

1. What is one fact about Daniel's life?
2. What is one example of an obstacle in Daniel's life?
3. What is a reason for that obstacle?
4. What is Daniel's dream or goal?

D Complete the chart with Daniel's obstacles and successes.

Daniel's obstacles	Daniel's successes
His parents died.	*He found a job in a local supermarket.*

E Plan a paragraph about a successful person you know. Use the chart to make notes on your own ideas.

_____'s obstacles	_____'s successes

2 Write

Write a paragraph about someone you know who is successful. Use the paragraph in Exercise 1B and the charts in Exercises 1D and 1E to help you.

3 After you write

A Check your writing.

	Yes	No
1. My topic sentence identifies a successful person.	☐	☐
2. I included examples of obstacles and successes.	☐	☐
3. I used active and passive verbs correctly.	☐	☐

B Share your writing with a partner.

1. Take turns. Read your paragraph to a partner.
2. Comment on your partner's paragraph. Ask your partner a question about the paragraph. Tell your partner one thing you learned.

Another view

1 Life-skills reading

Location of Vocational Classes

	North Center	South Center	West Center	Downtown Center	East Center
Auto Mechanics	■	■	■		
Certified Nursing Assistant	■	■	■	■	■
Food Service Worker	■	■	■		■
Hospitality and Tourism	■				
Office Systems	■	■	■		■
Retail		■		■	
Welding	■		■		
Workplace Readiness	■	■	■	■	■

A Read the questions. Look at the chart. Circle the answers.

1. Where are the most vocational classes offered?
   a. Downtown Center
   b. North Center
   c. South Center
   d. West Center

2. Where are the fewest vocational classes offered?
   a. Downtown Center
   b. North Center
   c. South Center
   d. West Center

3. Workplace Readiness is offered at which of the following sites?
   a. Downtown Center only
   b. East Center and West Center only
   c. North Center and South Center only
   d. all sites

4. Which vocational class is only offered at one site?
   a. Certified Nursing Assistant
   b. Hospitality and Tourism
   c. Retail
   d. Welding

5. You want to work in a hotel. Which class is appropriate for you?
   a. Hospitality and Tourism
   b. Office Systems
   c. Retail
   d. Welding

6. You want to study computers. Which class is appropriate for you?
   a. Auto Mechanics
   b. Food Service Worker
   c. Hospitality and Tourism
   d. Office Systems

B Talk with a partner. Ask and answer your own questions about the chart.

2 Fun with language

A Work in a small group. Complete the sentences with careers from the box. Discuss other successful people from your culture who are known for each of these careers.

ballet dancer	singer / actor	statesman
musician	soccer player	writer

1

Isabel Allende is known as a
_____*writer*_____ .

2

David Beckham is known as
a _____ .

3

Nelson Mandela is known
as a _____ .

4

Yo-Yo Ma is known as a
_____ .

5

Mikhail Baryshnikov is
known as a _____ .

6

Jennifer Lopez is known as
a _____ .

B Work with a partner. How many new words can you make with the letters from the phrase *plan for success*?

p-l-a-n   f-o-r   s-u-c-c-e-s-s

3 Wrap up

Complete the **Self-assessment** on page 141.

Review

1 Listening

🔘 **Listen.** Take notes on a conversation.

1. Type of certificate	*Automotive Technology*
2. Number of required classes	
3. Total number of courses	
4. Time to complete the program	
5. Cost per course	

Talk with a partner. Check your answers.

2 Grammar

A Write. Complete the story.

A Famous Athlete

Sammy Sosa ___*is considered*___ one of the world's great baseball players.
　　　　　　　　1. considers / is considered

Raised in the Dominican Republic, he was so _____ that he made a
　　　　　　　　　　　　　　　　　　　　　　　2. poor / poorly

bat out of a tree branch. After he picked up a real baseball bat at the age of 14, he

learned _____ . He had great kinesthetic intelligence. In 1989, he got
　　　3. quick / quickly

a contract with a major league baseball team. He didn't play _____ in
　　　　　　　　　　　　　　　　　　　　　　　　4. good / well

the beginning, but he hit 66 home runs in 1998. Sosa _____ for his
　　　　　　　　　　　　　　　　　　　　5. admires / is admired

generous donations to education and health in the Dominican Republic.

B Write. Look at the words that are underlined in the answers. Write
the questions.

1. **A** _____

   B Sammy Sosa grew up <u>in the Dominican Republic</u>.

2. **A** _____

   B He got a contract with the major leagues <u>in 1989</u>.

3. **A** _____

   B He is admired <u>for his generous donations</u>.

Talk with a partner. Ask and answer the questions.

3 Pronunciation: -ed verb endings

A 🎧 **Listen** to the -ed verb endings in these sentences.

/t/

1. He has always **liked** playing number games.
2. She has **worked** as an accountant for ten years.

/d/

3. Emily has **realized** that Brenda has a good brain.
4. Naturalists are **skilled** in working with plants.

/ɪd/

5. The little boy **started** counting when he was two.
6. She is **gifted** in singing and dancing.

🎧 **Listen again and repeat.** Pay attention to the -ed verb endings.

B 🎧 **Listen and repeat.** Then check (✓) the correct pronunciation for each -ed verb ending.

	/t/	/d/	/ɪd/
1. Classes are located at various elementary schools.			
2. All students are advised of the school rules.			
3. An application is required for admission.			
4. A math test is needed as well.			
5. The test is administered once a week.			
6. The students are expected to pay their fees soon.			
7. Lucas hasn't talked with a counselor yet.			
8. But he is finished with all his tests.			

Talk with a partner. Compare your answers.

C **Talk** with a partner. Practice the conversations. Pay attention to the pronunciation of the -ed verb endings: /t/, /d/, or /ɪd/.

1. *A* Are classes offered on Saturday?
   B Yes, classes are offered from 9:00 to 12:00.
2. *A* What are we expected to bring to class?
   B You are expected to bring a notebook, the textbook, and a pen.
3. *A* How did she cook?
   B She cooked very well.
4. *A* How did he paint?
   B He painted skillfully.

D **Write** five questions. Use the following words: *administered*, *required*, *located*, *expected*, and *provided*. Then ask your partner.

Friends and family

Lesson A *Get ready*

1 Talk about the pictures

A What do you see?
B What is happening?

Mary

Lan

Mrs. Lee

2 Listening

SELF-STUDY
AUDIO CD **A** 🔘 **Listen** and answer the questions.

1. Who are the speakers?
2. What are they talking about?

SELF-STUDY
AUDIO CD **B** 🔘 **Listen again.** Take notes.

Part 1	Part 2	Part 3
Reason for call: _Lan absent from class_ Action to take: _____	Mother's rules: _____ _____	Reason mother is upset: _____ Lan's punishment: _____

Listen again. Check your answers.

SELF-STUDY
AUDIO CD **C** 🔘 **Read.** Complete the story. Listen and check your answers.

bring (someone) up	chaperone	permitted	strict
broke (the) rules	grounded	raised	trust

Mrs. Lee received a phone message from her daughter's school saying Lan missed her 7th period class. Lan left school early to go to the mall with her friend Mary. At the mall, Lan tells Mary that her mother is too _____strict_____ .

                                                           1

Lan thinks it's because her mother wants to _____ her _____

                       2   2

the same way she was _____ in China. That's why Lan needs a

                             3

_____ to go out on a date. At home, Lan and her mother have an

        4

argument. Lan is angry because she's not _____ to go to the mall alone.

                                                    5

She thinks her mother doesn't _____ her. Mrs. Lee is upset because

                                         6

Lan _____ the _____ . As a punishment, she says Lan is

           7   7

_____ for two weeks.

    8

D Discuss. Talk with your classmates. Do you think Lan's mother is too strict? Give reasons for your opinion.

Culture note
When a child gets into trouble at school, the school staff calls the parents to help enforce the school rules.

Lesson B *Indirect questions*

1 Grammar focus: indirect *Wh-* questions

Direct *Wh-* questions

Why is she so strict?
How is everything at home?
Where did you go?
When did they leave?

Indirect *Wh-* questions

I wonder why she is so strict.
I'd like to know how everything is at home.
Can you tell me where you went?
Do you know when they left?

Introductory clauses

I'd like to know . . .   Tell me . . .   Can you tell me . . . ?
I don't know . . .   I wonder . . .   Do you know . . . ?

For a grammar explanation, turn to page 148.

2 Practice

A Write. Change the direct questions to indirect *Wh-* questions.

Culture note
Indirect questions are often more polite than direct questions. Use "please" to make the questions even more polite.

1. What is the student's name?

   A Do you know *what the student's name is* ?

   B Her name is Lan.

2. What class did she miss?

   A Can you please tell me _____ ?

   B Mr. Latham's 7th period English class.

3. Why did she break the rules?

   A I would like to know _____ .

   B I don't know why. Perhaps she was bored in class.

4. When did she and her friend leave the school?

   A I wonder _____ .

   B They left after 6th period.

5. What did they do at the mall?

   A I want to know _____ .

   B They talked and went window-shopping.

6. What was Lan's punishment?

   A Can you please tell me _____ ?

   B Her mother grounded her for two weeks.

Listen and check your answers. Then practice with a partner.

B **Talk** with a partner about Lan's report card. Ask indirect questions.

> *A* Do you know what grade Lan got in World History?
> *B* She got a B.

School Report Card – First Semester

Student's name: LAN SUZI LEE		Advisor: MR. GREEN
Subject	**Grade**	**Teacher**
WORLD HISTORY	B	LOPEZ
ADVANCED ENGLISH	A	LATHAM
ALGEBRA	B+	SMITH
P.E.	C	CHIN
CHEMISTRY	C	HOGAN
CERAMICS	A	AZARI

Write indirect questions about Lan's report card.

Do you know what grade Lan got in World History?

3 Communicate

A **Work** with a partner. Role-play conversations between a parent and a teenager. Use indirect questions with *who, what, where, when,* and *why.*

> *Parent* I'd like to know why you're late.
> *Teenager* I stayed after class to talk to my math teacher.
> *Parent* OK. But next time, call me if you're going to be late. All right?

Situation 1
The teenager is two hours late coming home from school.
The parent is worried.

Situation 2
The teenager's report card arrived in the mail. He or she got one A, two Bs, two Cs, and a D. Normally, the teenager gets all As and Bs. The parent is shocked.

B **Perform** your role play for the class.

Indirect questions

1 Grammar focus: indirect *Yes / No* questions

Direct *Yes / No* questions	Indirect *Yes / No* questions
Did you finish your homework?	I'd like to know if (whether) you finished your homework.
Do they have a test tomorrow?	Can you tell me if (whether) they have a test tomorrow?

For a grammar explanation, turn to page 148.

Useful language
In indirect *Yes / No* questions,
if = whether.

2 Practice

A Write. Complete the conversation. Use indirect *Yes / No* questions with *if*.

Son Can I go to a party at Joe's house?

Father Maybe. First I need to know ___*if you finished your homework*___ .
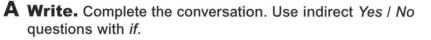
1. Did you finish your homework?

Son Yes, I finished it an hour ago.

Father OK. Can you tell me _____ ?
2. Will his parents be home?

Son Yes, his parents will be there.

Father That's good. I wonder _____ .
3. Do you need to take a birthday gift?

Son No, I don't. It's not a birthday party.

Father I wonder _____ .
4. Are they going to serve dinner?

Son Yes. They're going to barbecue chicken for us.

Father What about your friend John?

Do you know _____ ?
5. Is he invited to the party?

Son Yes, I think so.

Father Do you know _____ ?
6. Can John's parents bring you home?

Son I'll ask them.

🔘 **Listen** and check your answers. Then practice with a partner.

B Talk with a partner. Imagine you are a parent. Read the information you want to ask your daughter about the young man she is dating. Make indirect questions. Use a variety of introductory clauses.

> Can you tell me if he's a good student?

- is a good student
- has a job
- has nice friends
- has a good relationship with his parents

- lives alone or at home
- is polite
- drives carefully

Write the parents' indirect questions.

Can you tell me if he's a good student?

3 Communicate

A Work in a small group. Ask and answer questions about your lives when you were teenagers. Use indirect *Yes / No* questions. Discuss the items listed below.

- dating experience
- relationship with parents
- grades in school
- school activities
- things you were required to do at home
- things you were permitted to do
- things you weren't permitted to do

> *A* I'd like to know if you dated in high school.
> *B* Yes, I did. But only in a group.
> *C* I didn't date until after high school.

B Share information about your classmates.

1 Before you read

Talk with your classmates. Answer the questions.

1. How many generations of your family are living in the United States? Which generation are you?
2. What are some of the differences between you and the other generations in your family?
3. Look at the reading tip. Look up the meaning of *barrier*, and predict what the story will be about.

2 Read

SELF-STUDY
AUDIO CD

Read the magazine article. Listen and read again.

> Pay attention to words that repeat in a reading. They may give you an idea of what the reading is about.

Barriers Between Generations

In immigrant families, language differences and work schedules often create barriers to communication between the generations. Dolores Suarez, 42, and her son Diego, 16, face both kinds of barriers every day. Dolores is an immigrant from Mexico who works seven days a week as a housekeeper in a big hotel. She doesn't use much English in her job, and she has never had time to study it. Consequently, her English is limited. Her son, on the other hand, was raised in the United States. He understands Spanish, but he prefers to speak English. When his friends come over to visit, they speak only English. "They talk so fast, I can't understand what they are saying," says Dolores. To make the situation more complicated, Diego and Dolores live with Dolores's father, who speaks Nahuatl, a native language spoken in Mexico. Diego can't understand anything his grandfather says.

Dolores's work schedule is the second barrier to communication with Diego. Because she rarely has a day off, Dolores isn't able to spend much time with him. She doesn't have time to help him with his homework or attend parent-teacher conferences at his school. In 1995, when Dolores immigrated to the United States, her goal was to bring up her son with enough money to avoid the hardships her family suffered in Mexico. Her hard work has permitted Diego to have a comfortable life and a good education. But she has paid a price for this success. "Sometimes I feel like I don't know my own son," she says.

3 After you read

A Check your understanding.

1. What are the two barriers to communication between Dolores and her son?
2. Why is Dolores's English limited?
3. Which language does Diego prefer?
4. Why can't Diego communicate with his grandfather?
5. What was Dolores's goal when she came to the United States?
6. How do you think Dolores and her son could communicate better?

B Build your vocabulary.

1. Find and underline the following words in the reading: *immigrant, differences, create, communication, education,* and *success.*

2. Use a dictionary. Fill in the chart with the missing word forms.

Noun	Verb	Adjective
immigrant	*immigrate*	*immigrant*
differences		
	create	
communication		
education		
success		

3. Complete the sentences. Write the correct form of the word from Exercise B2.

a. My family decided to _____ to the United States because there was a war in my country.

b. Parents and teenagers almost always _____ in the kind of music they prefer.

c. Shosha paints beautiful and unusual oil paintings. She's very _____ .

d. Debra's son isn't very _____ . It's hard to know what he's thinking.

e. It's a parent's responsibility to _____ children about right and wrong behavior.

f. You need two things to be _____ in life: motivation and luck.

C Talk with a partner.

1. What are some ways that you and your parents are different?
2. How can parents help children to be more creative?
3. How can people communicate if they don't speak the same language?
4. Is it necessary to go to school to be an educated person? Explain your answer.

1 Before you write

A Talk with a partner. What are some differences between you and your parents or you and your children? Write your information in the charts.

Me	My parents
like salads and sandwiches	like lamb and rice

Me	My children
play cards	play video games

B Read the paragraph.

Different Eating Habits

One difference between my parents and me is that we don't have the same eating habits anymore. My family is Iranian, but I was brought up in the United States. Since most of my friends are American, I enjoy eating "American style." For example, I like to eat salads and sandwiches instead of meat and rice. Because of my job, I don't have time to cook, so I like fast food. I also love to eat in restaurants. On the other hand, my parents still eat like they did back home. They eat rice with every meal, and they eat a lot of lamb and vegetables. They don't like to eat in restaurants because my father thinks my mother is the best cook in the world. Actually, I agree with him. That's why I try to come home for dinner at least twice a week!

Transitions like *for example* and *on the other hand* show the relationship between sentences or ideas in a paragraph.

C Work with a partner. Complete the outline of the model paragraph.

Topic sentence: *One difference between my parents and me is that we don't have the same eating habits anymore.*

A Me: *I enjoy eating "American style."*

    1. Example: *I like to eat salads and sandwiches.*

    2. Example: *I don't eat a lot of meat and rice.*

    3. Example: *I like fast food.*

Transition: *On the other hand*

B My parents: _____

    1. Example: _____

    2. Example: _____

    3. Example: _____

D Plan a paragraph about a difference between you and your parents or you and your children. Include examples to support your main idea. Make an outline. Use your own paper.

2 Write

Write a paragraph about a difference between you and your parents or you and your children. Use the paragraph in Exercise 1B and the outlines in Exercises 1C and 1D to help you.

3 After you write

A Check your writing.

	Yes	No
1. My topic sentence states the difference between my parents and me or my children and me.	☐	☐
2. I gave examples to support the main idea.	☐	☐
3. I used a transition between the two parts of my paragraph.	☐	☐

B Share your writing with a partner.

1. Take turns. Read your paragraph to a partner.
2. Comment on your partner's paragraph. Ask your partner a question about the paragraph. Tell your partner one thing you learned.

Another view

1 Life-skills reading

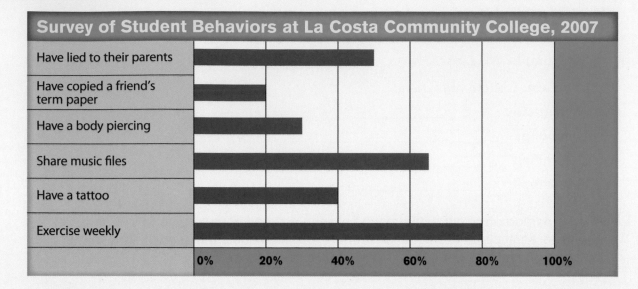

Survey of Student Behaviors at La Costa Community College, 2007

	0%	20%	40%	60%	80%	100%
Have lied to their parents						
Have copied a friend's term paper						
Have a body piercing						
Share music files						
Have a tattoo						
Exercise weekly						

A Read the questions. Look at the survey results. Circle the answers.

1. What was the population surveyed in this study?
   a. high school students
   b. college students
   c. adult school students
   d. none of the above

2. What percentage of the people in the survey said they exercise weekly?
   a. 35%
   b. 40%
   c. 65%
   d. 80%

3. What percentage of the people in the survey have a tattoo?
   a. 10%
   b. 35%
   c. 40%
   d. 65%

4. According to the survey, the highest percentage of students _____ .
   a. exercise weekly
   b. have lied to their parents
   c. share music files
   d. have copied a friend's term paper

5. According to the survey, the lowest percentage of students _____ .
   a. have copied a term paper
   b. have a body piercing
   c. have a tattoo
   d. have lied to their parents

6. Which of the following statements is true?
   a. More students share music files than exercise weekly.
   b. More students have a body piercing than a tattoo.
   c. More students have copied a friend's term paper than lied to their parents.
   d. More students have a tattoo than a body piercing.

B Talk with a partner. What do you think about these survey results? Does anything surprise you?

2 Fun with language

A Work with a partner. Pretend you have a 16-year-old daughter and a 16-year-old son. What would you permit her or him to do? Complete the survey for yourself. Then interview a classmate.

	You		Your partner: _____	
	Daughter Yes / No	Son Yes / No	Daughter Yes / No	Son Yes / No
1. go to the mall with friends				
2. go out on a date with no chaperone				
3. spend the night at a friend's house				
4. stay out after midnight				
5. get a tattoo				
6. get a body piercing				
7. get a driver's license				
8. have a cell phone				
9. dye hair a strange color				
10. wear the same clothes other teenagers are wearing				

B Work in a group. Compare your responses. Choose two or three interesting results and report them to the class. What conclusions can you make about generational differences or cultural differences among students in your class?

3 Wrap up

Complete the **Self-assessment** on page 142.

Lesson A Get ready

1 Talk about the pictures

A What do you see?

B What is happening?

2 Listening

SELF-STUDY AUDIO CD **A** **Listen** and answer the questions.

1. Who are the speakers?
2. What are they talking about?

SELF-STUDY AUDIO CD **B** **Listen again.** Complete the chart.

Sara's symptoms	Mike's advice
1. *can't sleep*	4.
2.	5.
3.	6.

Listen again. Check your answers.

SELF-STUDY AUDIO CD **C** **Read.** Complete the story. Listen and check your answers.

anxiety	calm down	cope with	stressed out
breathing	concentrate	meditation	tense

Mike is driving Sara to the Department of Motor Vehicles (DMV) to take her driving test. He notices that she's very ___ *tense* ___ .
1
Sara says she's ___ because she was late to work again.
2
She's worried that her boss will fire her if she's late one more time. She's so afraid of losing her job that she can't eat, she can't sleep, and she can't ___ . Mike says that she has to ___
3   4
if she wants to pass her driving test. He suggests three techniques to help her ___ her ___ . One is deep
5   6
___ . The second one is thinking positive thoughts, and
7
the third one is ___ .
8

D **Discuss.** Talk with your classmates.

1. Do you ever feel stressed out? What are your symptoms?
2. What helps you when you feel stressed?

Lesson B Modals

1 Grammar focus: *ought to, shouldn't, have to, don't have to*

Advice

Sara ought to learn how to meditate.
She shouldn't get stressed out.

Necessity

Sara has to take public transportation
because she doesn't have a car.

Lack of necessity

She doesn't have to take her driving
test today. She can take it next week.

For a grammar explanation, turn to page 148.

Useful language
ought to = should

2 Practice

A Write. Complete the story. Use *ought to*, *shouldn't*, *have to*, and *don't have to*.

Ana and Bill just got engaged, and they are planning to get married in four weeks. Because the wedding is so soon, they are feeling a lot of pressure. Ana's mother wants a big wedding, but Ana and Bill don't. Because they are paying for the wedding themselves, they believe they ___ought to___ do
  ₁
what they want. Another pressure is all the things Ana and Bill

_____ do before the wedding. For example, Ana _____ buy
          2   3
a dress, choose her bridesmaids, and send out the invitations. Bill _____
                                                                                  4
plan the reception and order the food. Most importantly, they _____
                                                                        5
decide where the wedding will be. Ana wants to get married outdoors, but Bill thinks

they _____ plan an outdoor wedding because it might rain. Now Bill
                6
has a different idea. He realizes that they _____ get married so soon.
                                                          7
Maybe they _____ postpone the wedding until the spring. That way, they
                      8
_____ feel so much pressure.
        9

 **Listen** and check your answers.

B Talk with a partner. Discuss what the people in the pictures *ought to*, *shouldn't*, *have to*, and *don't have to* do. Use the items from the box in your discussion.

> Carmela and Hugo ought to try to meet new people.

> Kevin doesn't have to follow his parents' advice.

Carmela and Hugo
- just got married
- just moved to a new town

Chul and Sun Mi
- just had a baby
- live in a studio apartment

Kevin
- just started his first job
- still lives with his parents

try to meet new people	ask lots of questions
call parents whenever they have (he has) a problem	find a new place to live
	follow their (his) parents' advice
learn how to manage money	make decisions by themselves (himself)
try to do everything perfectly	be responsible

Write sentences about the people in the pictures.

Carmela and Hugo ought to try to meet new people.

3 Communicate

A Work in a small group. Discuss the following situations, and give advice. Use *ought to*, *shouldn't*, *have to*, and *don't have to*.

1. The Wong family has just bought a house. The house has no furniture at all. Also, it is far from Mr. Wong's job, and the family doesn't have a car.

> They have to buy furniture.

> They ought to check the newspaper for furniture sales.

2. Etsuko and Hiro have just immigrated to the United States. They are anxious because there are so many things to do. They don't have a big enough place to live, they aren't enrolled in English classes, and their children aren't registered for school.

3. Boris is very nervous about his new job. He doesn't know anyone at the company yet, and he doesn't know his duties yet, either. His boss is a woman. He has never worked for a woman before.

B Share your group's advice with your classmates.

Lesson C Modals

1 Grammar focus: *should have, shouldn't have*

Regret in the past	Advice in the past
I hate my new job.	Robert is late to work.
I should have kept my old job.	He should have left the house earlier.
I shouldn't have changed jobs.	He shouldn't have read the newspaper before work.

For a grammar explanation, turn to page 149.
For a list of past participles, turn to page 154.

2 Practice

A Write. Read about Imelda. Write sentences with *should have* and *shouldn't have*.

Imelda left the Philippines last year and immigrated to the United States. None of her family came with her. She got homesick and depressed.

1. She didn't talk to anyone about her problems.
   She should have talked to someone about her problems.

2. She didn't go out.
   _____

3. She stayed home alone all the time.
   _____

4. She didn't make new friends.
   _____

5. She didn't exercise.
   _____

6. She didn't eat regular, balanced meals.
   _____

7. She ate lots of junk food.
   _____

8. She slept a lot.
   _____

9. She didn't call her family.
   _____

   Listen and check your answers.

B Talk with a partner. Look at the pictures. What should Nikolai and his boss have done differently? Use *shouldn't have*.

Nikolai shouldn't have overslept.

oversleep

forget (one's) briefcase

arrive late

criticize (someone) in public

leave the meeting

lose (one's) temper

Write sentences about what Nikolai and his boss should have done instead.

Nikolai should have gotten up on time.

3 Communicate

A Work in a small group. Think about a past situation in your life that didn't go well. Take turns asking and answering questions about it.

1. What was the situation?
2. What did you do that you shouldn't have?
3. What didn't you do that you should have?

B Share information about your classmates.

1 Before you read

Talk with your classmates. Answer the questions.

1. When you are in a stressful situation, what happens to your body?
2. Read the **boldfaced** questions in the article. Share your answers to these questions before you read the article.

2 Read

SELF-STUDY
AUDIO CD   **Read** the magazine article. Listen and read again.

STRESS:
What You Ought to Know

What is stress?

Stress is our reaction to changing events in our lives. The reactions can be mental – what we *think* or *feel* about the changes – and physical – how our body *reacts* to the changes.

What causes stress?

Stress often comes when there are too many changes in our lives. The changes can be positive, like having a baby or getting a better job, or they can be negative, such as an illness or a divorce. Some stress is healthy. It motivates us to push forward. But too much stress over time can make us sick.

What are the signs of stress?

There are both physical and emotional signs of stress. Physical signs may include tight muscles, elevated blood pressure, grinding your teeth, trouble sleeping, an upset stomach, and back pain. Common emotional symptoms are anxiety, nervousness, depression, trouble concentrating, and nightmares.

How can you manage stress?

To prevent stress, you should eat right and exercise regularly. When you know there will be a stressful event in your day – such as a test, a business meeting, or an encounter with someone you don't get along with – it is really important to eat a healthy breakfast and to limit coffee and sugar.

When you find yourself in a stressful situation, stay calm. Take a few deep breaths to help you relax. Roll your shoulders or stretch to loosen any tight muscles. And take time to think before you speak. You don't want to say something you will regret later!

3 After you read

A Check your understanding.

1. What are some physical signs of stress?
2. What are some emotional signs of stress?
3. What should you eat when you know there will be a stressful event in your life? What foods should you avoid?
4. Do you have a favorite exercise that you do to reduce stress? If so, what is it?
5. Think of a time when there were many changes in your life. Were the changes positive or negative? How did you feel? How did your body react?

> Good readers relate what they are reading to their own experience.

B Build your vocabulary.

1. English uses suffixes to change the part of speech of a word. Underline words in the reading that end with the suffixes in the left column.

2. Complete the chart. Use a dictionary if necessary.

Suffix	Example	Part of speech	Main word	Part of speech
-ful	stressful	adj	stress	noun
-en				
-ly				
-ness				
-ion				

3. Work with a partner. Compare the examples from the reading with the main words. How does each suffix change the main word?

   The suffix -ful changes a noun to an adjective.

4. Work with a partner. On your own paper, write more words with each suffix. Write a sentence for each new word.

C Talk with a partner.

1. What's a stressful situation you've been in recently?
2. Why is it important to exercise regularly?
3. What are some physical habits that can show nervousness?
4. Is it a good idea to take medicine for depression? Why or why not?
5. Do your muscles often get tight? How do you loosen them?

1 Before you write

A **Talk** with a partner. Look at the pictures. Answer the questions.

1. How do the people in the pictures cope with stress?
2. What are some healthy ways of coping with stress?
3. What are some unhealthy ways of coping with stress?
4. What makes you feel stressed?

B **Read** the paragraph.

> *How I Cope with Stress*
>
> When I feel stressed, I like to curl up with my cat, listen to classical music, and read an interesting book. Stroking my cat's soft fur helps my body relax, and soon I feel less tense. The sound of classical music with piano and string instruments shuts out the noises around me and reduces my anxiety. I like to listen with my eyes closed until my muscles start to relax. Then I open my eyes and pick up a book. I usually choose stories about people and the difficult events in their lives because they help me forget about all the stressful things I have to do in my own life.

One way to organize details in a paragraph is to write about actions and the results of those actions.

I like to listen with my eyes closed (action) *until my muscles start to relax* (result).

C Work with a partner. Complete the outline of the model paragraph.

Topic sentence: When I feel stressed, _____

_____ .

Ways of reducing stress:

action: *stroke my cat's fur*   →   result: *body relaxes, feel less tense*

action: _____ →   result: _____

action: _____ →   result: _____

D Plan a paragraph about how you cope with stress. Use the outline to make notes on your ideas.

Topic sentence: When I feel stressed, _____

_____ .

Ways of reducing stress:

action: _____ →   result: _____

action: _____ →   result: _____

action: _____ →   result: _____

2 Write

Write a paragraph about how you cope with stress. Use the paragraph in Exercise 1B and the outlines in Exercises 1C and 1D to help you.

3 After you write

A Check your writing.

	Yes	No
1. My topic sentence identifies actions for coping with stress.	☐	☐
2. For each action, I described a result.	☐	☐
3. I used modals and verb tenses correctly.	☐	☐

B Share your writing with a partner.

1. Take turns. Read your paragraph to a partner.
2. Comment on your partner's paragraph. Ask your partner a question about the paragraph. Tell your partner one thing you learned.

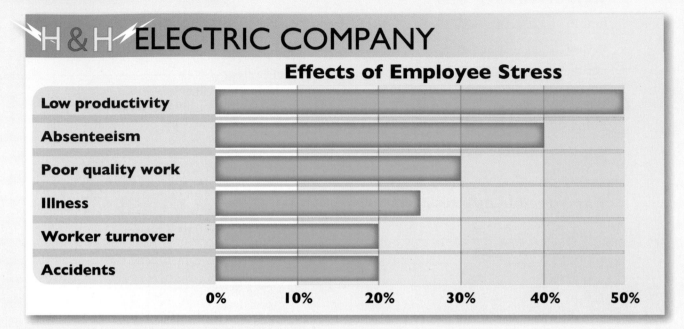

A Read the questions. Look at the bar graph. Circle the answers.

1. This chart is about _____ .
   a. how stress affects employees
   b. how stress affects a business
   c. both a and b
   d. neither a nor b

2. Employee stress is the cause of _____ .
   a. 30 percent of poor quality work
   b. 20 percent of worker turnover
   c. both a and b
   d. neither a nor b

3. Employee stress contributes to worker turnover less than it contributes to _____ .
   a. productivity
   b. work quality
   c. illness
   d. all of the above

4. Employee stress affects accidents as much as it affects _____ .
   a. absenteeism
   b. worker turnover
   c. both a and b
   d. neither a nor b

5. Employee stress affects _____ the most.
   a. productivity
   b. work quality
   c. illness
   d. absenteeism

6. Employee stress affects illness more than it affects _____ .
   a. productivity
   b. absenteeism
   c. both a and b
   d. neither a nor b

B Talk with your classmates. Should employers do something to relieve stress in the workplace? Why or why not? What could they do?

2 Fun with language

A Write your answers to this test about stress.

STRESS TEST

*Directions: Give each statement a score of 1 to 5 to indicate
how true the statement is about you.*
1 = Always   2 = Often   3 = Sometimes   4 = Rarely   5 = Never

1. I eat at least one balanced meal a day. _____

2. I get seven to eight hours of sleep a night. _____

3. I am in good health. _____

4. I am the correct weight for my height. _____

5. I have fewer than three caffeinated drinks (coffee, tea, or soda) a day. _____

6. I have enough money to pay for necessary things. _____

7. I have someone I talk to when I have personal problems. _____

8. When I am angry or worried, I am able to talk about it. _____

9. I organize my time effectively. _____

10. I make some time for myself each day. _____

11. I do something for fun at least once a week. _____

12. I exercise or walk at least three times a week. _____

Total _____

Add the numbers in the right-hand column. How much stress do you have?
Little or no stress 12–24   A lot of stress 37–48
Some stress 25–36   Too much stress 49–60

B Talk with your classmates about your test results.

1. How much stress do you have in your life?
2. Is there anything you ought to change? If so, what?
3. Is there anything you don't have to change? If not, why not?

3 Wrap up

Complete the **Self-assessment** on page 142.

Review

1 Listening

🔘 **Listen.** Take notes on a phone conversation.

Yesenia's symptoms	Sue's suggestions
1. *tense*	4.
2.	5.
3.	6.

Talk with a partner. Check your answers.

2 Grammar

A Write. Complete the story. Use indirect questions.

Ann's Night Out

Ann is 16 years old. It's midnight, and she isn't home yet. She went out

with her friend Liz. Ann's mom doesn't know _____*where they went*_____ . She
1. Where did they go?

wonders _____ . Ann's mother wants to call Liz's house, but
2. Are Ann and Liz safe?

she doesn't know _____ . Ann's father is worried, too. He
3. What is the phone number?

wonders _____ . Then he hears a sound. For a minute, he
4. Can he find them?

doesn't know _____ . It's Ann! Her father says, "We had no
5. Who is it?

idea _____ , but we're glad you're home."
6. Where were you?

B Write. Look at the words that are underlined in the answers. Write
the questions.

1. **A** _____

   B Ann should have been home <u>at 11:00</u>.

2. **A** _____

   B She should have called <u>her parents</u>.

3. **A** _____

   B Ann's parents should <u>ground her</u>.

Talk with a partner. Ask and answer the questions.

3 Pronunciation: intonation in questions

A 💿 **Listen** to the intonation in these questions.

Direct question   **Indirect question**

Where did he go?   Can you tell me where he went?

💿 **Listen again and repeat.** Pay attention to the intonation.

B 💿 **Listen and repeat.** Then draw arrows to show rising or falling intonation in the questions.

1. **A** What does Ann do to reduce stress?
   B She listens to music.

2. **A** Why are you so tense?
   B I have my driver's test today.

3. **A** Do you know what Rodolfo does to calm down?
   B He walks or jogs.

4. **A** When did Ivan miss his class?
   B He missed his class on Tuesday.

5. **A** Can you tell me where Andy lives?
   B He lives on East Fifth Street.

6. **A** Do you know why they're always late?
   B No, I don't know.

Talk with a partner. Compare your answers.

C **Talk** with a partner. Ask and answer the questions. Use the correct intonation.

1. What is one thing you should have done today or yesterday?
2. What is a common punishment for teenagers when they come home late?
3. What were your favorite things to do when you were growing up?
4. Can you tell me what you do to reduce stress?
5. Do you know why it's important to exercise regularly?
6. Do you know if meditation is difficult to do?

D **Write** five questions. Make at least three indirect questions. Ask your partner.

Can you tell me how you cope with stressful situations?

1. _____
2. _____
3. _____
4. _____
5. _____

Lesson A *Get ready*

1 Talk about the pictures

A What do you see?

B What is happening?

2 Listening

SELF-STUDY
AUDIO CD **A** **Listen** and answer the questions.

1. Who are the speakers?
2. What are they talking about?

SELF-STUDY
AUDIO CD **B** **Listen again.** Complete the chart.

Almaz's responsibilities at the library	Volunteer responsibilities at Quiet Palms
1. *worked with adults learning to read*	4.
2.	5.
3.	6.

Listen again. Check your answers.

SELF-STUDY
AUDIO CD **C** **Read.** Complete the story. Listen and check your answers.

can't wait	compassionate	orientation	residents
commitment	coordinator	patient	worthwhile

Last summer, Almaz volunteered at the public library downtown. She liked working with the older people because she felt that she was doing something ____worthwhile____ . Today, she is meeting with Steve, the volunteer
1
_____ at Quiet Palms, a nursing home. She wants to volunteer
2
there to find out if she likes working in the health-care field. Steve tells her about some of her responsibilities at Quiet Palms. He says it's very important for volunteers to be _____ and _____ when
3 4
they are working with the _____ . He asks Almaz to make a
5
_____ to volunteer at least three hours per week. Almaz agrees
6
to attend an _____ . She says she _____ to
7 8
start volunteering.

D **Discuss.** Talk with your classmates. Is the nursing home a good place for Almaz to volunteer? Why or why not?

Culture note
A *nursing home* is a place where elderly people live when their families can't take care of them.

Lesson B Time clauses

1 Grammar focus: clauses with *until* and *as soon as*

Almaz will stay with Mr. Shamash until he finishes his lunch.
Until Mr. Shamash finishes his lunch, Almaz will stay with him.

Almaz will leave Quiet Palms as soon as Mr. Shamash finishes his lunch.
As soon as Mr. Shamash finishes his lunch, Almaz will leave Quiet Palms.

For a grammar explanation, turn to page 149.

2 Practice

A Write. Complete the sentences with *until* or *as soon as*.

1. **A** Mr. Shamash is in pain. When will he start to feel better?

   B He'll feel better ____as soon as____ he takes his medication.

2. **A** How long will Mr. Shamash stay at Quiet Palms?

   B He'll stay _____ his broken hip heals.

3. **A** When can Mr. Shamash begin exercising again?

   B _____ Mr. Shamash feels stronger, he can start doing moderate exercise.

4. **A** When does Mr. Shamash get ready for his walk?

   B He gets ready _____ Almaz arrives.

5. **A** How long will Mr. Shamash and Almaz play cards?

   B They'll play cards _____ it is time for lunch.

6. **A** How long will Almaz stay with Mr. Shamash?

   B She'll stay _____ his family arrives to visit him.

7. **A** When is Mr. Shamash going to go to sleep?

   B _____ his visitors leave, he'll take his medicine and go to sleep.

   Listen and check your answers. Then practice with a partner.

B **Talk** with a partner. Discuss Charles's volunteer activities at another nursing home. Use *as soon as* or *until*.

> As soon as Charles arrives at work, he puts on his name tag.

1 arrive / put on name tag

2 walk with Mrs. Halliday / time to deliver mail

3 read to Mrs. Halliday / lunchtime

4 stop reading / lunch is delivered

5 talk to Mrs. Halliday / finish eating

6 go home / finish playing a game with Mrs. Halliday

Write sentences about Charles's volunteer activities.

As soon as Charles arrives at work, he puts on his name tag.

Culture note
Volunteering is a popular activity among Americans of all ages, from children to senior citizens.

3 Communicate

A **Choose** one time when you helped someone or volunteered. Make a list of your activities. Use Exercise 2B to help you.

B **Work** with a partner. Ask questions about each other's activities. Use *as soon as* and *until*.

> **A** What did you do as soon as you arrived at the animal shelter?
> **B** I checked the board for my duties.
> **A** How late did you stay?
> **B** I stayed until the shelter closed for the day.

C **Share** information about your partner.

Verb tense contrast

1 Grammar focus: repeated actions in the present and past

	Number of times	Time expressions
Sana volunteers at the homeless shelter		a week. each month.
Sana has volunteered at the homeless shelter	once twice three times several times many times	so far. until now. in her life.
Sana volunteered at the homeless shelter		each month. last year. two years ago. when she was 12.

For a grammar explanation, turn to page 149.

2 Practice

A Write. Complete the story with the present, present perfect, or past forms of the verbs.

Sharing with Sally

Sally Sutherland created "Sharing with Sally," a volunteer organization that helps seniors stay connected with the outside world. The organization __has delivered__ over 5,000
1. deliver
dinners to seniors so far. Sharing with Sally

_____ six years ago. Every week, Sally and her volunteers _____
2. begin 3. deliver
meals, _____ to seniors on the phone, and _____ the ones who
4. talk 5. visit
can't leave their homes. Over 200 people volunteer at Sharing with Sally. Jake, a

college student, _____ all last year. He _____ elderly people on the
6. volunteer 7. call
phone once a week and _____ to each person. He said it was a very valuable
8. talk
experience. Betsy, a 35-year-old mother of two, _____ for two years so far and
9. volunteer
loves it.

Listen and check your answers.

B Talk with a partner. Make sentences about Betsy's volunteer experience. Include the number of times and time expressions.

> **A** Betsy visited seniors at their homes 30 times last year.
> **B** And she's visited them 15 times so far this year.

Activity	Number of times last year	Number of times this year
Visit seniors at their homes	30	15
Deliver meals	25	10
Call seniors on the phone	45	25
Help Sally put meals in the truck	5	1
Take her children with her to the seniors' homes	10	3

Write sentences about Betsy's activities.

Betsy visited seniors at their homes 30 times last year.

3 Communicate

A Make a list of your experiences volunteering or helping people.

Last year	This year
• *took my grandmother to the hairdresser*	• *babysit my nephew while my sister is at work*
• _____	• _____
• _____	• _____
• _____	• _____

B Work with a partner. Share your lists. Ask questions about your partner's activities. Use *How often . . . ?* or *How many times . . . ?*

> **A** How often did you take your grandmother to the hairdresser last year?
> **B** I took her every week.
> **A** How many times a week do you babysit your nephew?
> **B** I babysit once or twice a week.
> **A** How many times have you babysat your nephew so far?
> **B** About six times so far this year.

C Share information about your partner.

1 Before you read

Talk with your classmates. Answer the questions.

1. Look at the picture. What is unusual about it?
2. Read the title. What do you think the story will be about?

2 Read

SELF-STUDY
AUDIO CD **Read** the newspaper article. Listen and read again.

A WORTHWHILE COMMITMENT

Imagine running with your eyes closed. How do you feel? Insecure? Afraid? Justin Andrews knows these feelings very well. Justin is a former long-distance runner who lost his vision because of a grave illness. For the past six months, he has been running twice a week with the help of volunteer runners at Running with Ropes, an organization that assists blind and visually impaired runners. "Running with Ropes has changed my life," Justin says. "Until I heard about it, I thought I'd never run outside again."

Volunteers at Running with Ropes make a commitment to volunteer two to four hours a week. Scott Liponi, one of the running volunteers, explains what they do. "We use ropes to join ourselves to the blind runners and guide them around and over obstacles, such as holes in the road and other runners." Scott has learned how to keep the rope loose so the blind runner has more freedom. He deeply respects the blind runners' tenacity. "They are incredibly determined," he says. "It doesn't matter if it's hot, raining, or snowing – they are going to run." Scott says it is gratifying to share in the joy of the runners and to feel that they trust him. "The four hours I spend at Running with Ropes are the most rewarding part of my week," he says. "It's really a worthwhile commitment."

3 After you read

A Check your understanding.

1. Who is Justin Andrews? What happened to him?
2. What is Running with Ropes?
3. How is Justin able to run?
4. Who is Scott Liponi?
5. How does Scott feel about his volunteer commitment?

> When you see a new word, look at the words around it to guess if the meaning is positive or negative.
>
> *He lost his vision because of a* **grave** *illness.*
>
> You can guess that *grave* has a negative meaning.

B Build your vocabulary.

1. Look at the reading tip. Then underline the words from the chart in the reading passage. Decide if their meanings are positive or negative. Fill in the clues that helped you guess.

Word	Positive	Negative	Clue
1. grave		✓	*He lost his vision because of an illness.*
2. insecure			
3. impaired			
4. freedom			
5. tenacity			
6. gratifying			
7. rewarding			

2. Work with your classmates. Write four more words in the reading that have a positive or negative meaning. Write *P* next to positive words. Write *N* next to negative words.

a. _____   c. _____

b. _____   d. _____

C Talk with a partner.

1. When do you feel most insecure?
2. Tell about something that takes tenacity.
3. Describe a gratifying experience.
4. What do visually impaired people use to help them? What about hearing-impaired people?

Lesson E Writing

1 Before you write

A Talk with your classmates. Look at the picture. Answer the questions.

1. Who are the people in the picture? Where are they? What are they doing?
2. Do you think the young woman is doing something unusual? Why or why not?

B Read the paragraph.

> ### Story Lady
>
> My friend Vivianne is one of the most compassionate people I have ever met. After college, she wanted to do something truly worthwhile, so she spent a year working as a literacy volunteer in northeastern Brazil. At the time, this area didn't have any libraries, so Vivianne traveled to different schools in a mobile library van. As soon as she arrived at a school, the children would run outside and shout, "Story Lady! Story Lady!" Then everyone went inside, sat down, and listened quietly while she read them a story. Vivianne made a huge difference in these children's lives. She introduced them to literature and taught them to love reading. Today, she still gets letters from children who remember her generosity and kindness.

Make your writing more interesting by including specific details that answer the questions *who, what, when, where, why,* and *how*.

C Work with a partner. Write the words *who, when, where, why, what,* or *how* next to the details from the paragraph.

1. _____*who*_____ my friend Vivianne
2. _____ after college
3. _____ a literacy volunteer
4. _____ northeastern Brazil
5. _____ because the area didn't have any libraries
6. _____ in a mobile library van
7. _____ She read stories to the children.
8. _____ She introduced them to literature and taught them to love reading.

D Plan a paragraph about someone you know who made a difference. Use the chart to make notes.

Who made a difference?	
What did he or she do?	
Why did this person do it?	
Where did it happen?	
When did it happen?	
How did this person make a difference?	

2 Write

Write a paragraph about someone you know who made a difference. Use the paragraph in Exercise 1B and the chart in Exercise 1D to help you.

3 After you write

A Check your writing.

	Yes	No
1. My topic sentence names the person who made a difference.	☐	☐
2. I included details that answer *Wh-* questions.	☐	☐
3. I used verb tenses correctly with time words and expressions.	☐	☐

B Share your writing with a partner.

1. Take turns. Read your paragraph to a partner.
2. Comment on your partner's paragraph. Ask your partner a question about the paragraph. Tell your partner one thing you learned.

Another view

1 Life-skills reading

Want to get involved?
Volunteer opportunities are listed every Wednesday.

1 HEALTH
Agency: San Antonio Meals for Seniors
Need: Volunteers to drive meals to seniors' homes
Contact: Jim Jefferies, 555-2324

Site: Downtown area
Time commitment: 3 hours per week

2 LITERACY
Agency: San Antonio Literacy Foundation
Need: Volunteers to tutor basic reading, writing, and math skills to adults
Contact: 555-3131

Site: Around the city
Time commitment: 4 hours per week, 3-month commitment, plus 12 hours training

3 ANIMALS
Agency: "Make People Smile" Animal Therapy
Need: Volunteers and their pets to visit hospitals and nursing homes
Contact: Judy, Jsmith@mpsat.org

Site: Throughout the county
Time commitment: 4 hours per month

4 GENERAL ADMINISTRATION
Agency: San Antonio Zoo
Need: Volunteers to help with mailings and other office jobs; assist various departments, including administration, marketing, and membership
Contact: Tina de la Peña, 555-5432

Site: Zoo's administration building
Time commitment: Flexible

A Read the questions. Look at the advertisements for volunteer positions. Circle the answers.

1. Which volunteer position requires the biggest time commitment?
   a. 1   c. 3
   b. 2   d. 4

2. Which ad wants you to e-mail your response?
   a. 1   c. 3
   b. 2   d. 4

3. Which position requires math skills?
   a. 1   c. 3
   b. 2   d. none of the positions

4. Which position requires office skills?
   a. 1   c. 3
   b. 2   d. 4

5. Which position requires a driver's license?
   a. 1   c. 3
   b. 2   d. 4

6. Which position requires some training?
   a. 1   c. 3
   b. 2   d. none of the positions

B Talk with your classmates. Discuss the ads. Which ones are interesting to you? Why?

2 Fun with language

A Work in a group. Read the list of popular sayings about giving. Discuss the meanings. Then look at the pictures. Match the sayings with the pictures.

a. From small beginnings come great things.
b. Many hands make light work.
c. The best things in life are free.
d. It's better to give than to get.

1. _c_
2. _____
3. _____
4. _____

B Talk with your classmates. Find someone who has volunteered to do the activities in the chart.

Find someone who has volunteered . . .	Name
to serve food to homeless people	*Hector*
to play music for others	
to tutor a child	
to coach a team	
to sell items to raise money for charity	
to help elderly people	

Share information about your classmates.

3 Wrap up

Complete the **Self-assessment** on page 143.

Lesson A *Get ready*

1 Talk about the pictures

A What do you see?
B What is happening?

Mrs. Rosen

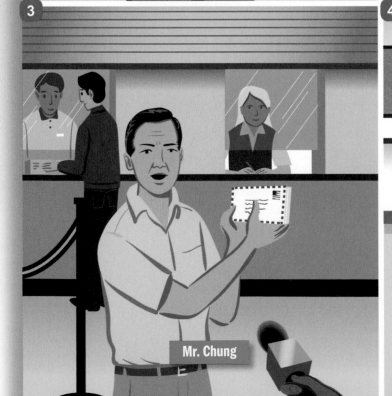

Mr. Chung

Ms. Morales

Mail

2 Listening

SELF-STUDY
AUDIO CD **A** 🔊 **Listen** and answer the questions.

    1. Who are the speakers?

    2. What are they talking about?

SELF-STUDY
AUDIO CD **B** 🔊 **Listen again.** Complete the chart.

	Time-saving device	Opinion about time-saving device
1. Mrs. Rosen	*address stamper*	
2. Mr. Chung		
3. Ms. Morales		

Listen again. Check your answers.

SELF-STUDY
AUDIO CD **C** 🔊 **Read.** Complete the story. Listen and check your answers.

convenient	distracting	innovative	spam
devices	electronic	manual	text message

       Today, a reporter from KESL Radio asked three people about technology

and their favorite time-saving _____*devices*_____ . Mrs. Rosen's favorite

                  1

device is _____ . She says it saves time, even though it isn't

            2

_____ . Mr. Chung isn't a fan of technology. In fact, he says

      3

technology wastes more time than it saves. For example, he says he doesn't like

e-mail because he gets lots of _____ . He also finds e-mail

                        4

_____ . He doesn't think it is _____ .

    5   6

Ms. Morales loves technology. She uses the camera on her cell phone in a very

_____ way – to send her daughter pictures of clothes that

      7

are on sale. Her daughter sends a _____ back: "Buy" or

                            8

"Don't buy."

D Discuss. Talk with a partner.

    1. Do you agree with the people interviewed? Why or why not?

    2. In general, do you think technology saves time or wastes time? Give
       examples.

Clauses of concession

1 Grammar focus: *although, even though*

> Although (Even though) e-mail is fast, Mr. Chung doesn't like to use it.
> Mr. Chung doesn't like to use e-mail although (even though) it is fast.
>
> *For a grammar explanation, turn to page 150.*

2 Practice

A Write. Combine the sentences. Use *even though*.

1. Mr. Gormet doesn't want a microwave. He knows microwaves save time.

   Mr. Gormet doesn't want a microwave even though he knows they save time.

2. Ms. Honig's car has a GPS system. She gets lost all the time.

3. Mr. Wang doesn't have a laptop computer. He travels constantly.

4. Mrs. Sanchez can't operate her digital camera. She read the instructions three times.

5. Mrs. Belcanto doesn't want a dishwasher. She has six children.

6. Ms. Kaye had urgent business in another state. She refused to travel by plane.

7. My house has central air-conditioning. I prefer to use a fan when it's hot.

8. My grandmother doesn't use e-mail. She has an e-mail address.

9. DVD movies are very popular. I still watch movies on videocassettes.

Listen and check your answers.

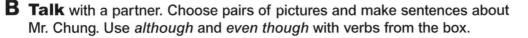

B Talk with a partner. Choose pairs of pictures and make sentences about Mr. Chung. Use *although* and *even though* with verbs from the box.

| clean | find information | have | listen | use | wash | write |

> Although Mr. Chung has a computer, he prefers to write letters by hand.

Write sentences about Mr. Chung.

Although Mr. Chung has a computer, he prefers to write letters by hand.

3 Communicate

A Work in a small group. Talk about time-saving devices or tools that you own but don't use. Use *although* and *even though*.

> **A** Although I have a food processor, I almost never use it.
> **B** Why?
> **A** It's too hard to clean.

Culture note

In the United States, many people hold garage or yard sales to sell their household items that they no longer use.

B Share information about your classmates.

Clauses of reason and concession

1 Grammar focus: contrasting *because* and *although*

> Because wireless technology is fast, many schools have it.
> Although wireless technology is fast, my school cannot afford it.
>
> *For a grammar explanation, turn to page 150.*

2 Practice

A Write. Complete the story. Use *because* or *although*.

Pam

Beth

___*Although*___ Pam and Beth are sisters, they are very different. Pam is
     1
very modern. She loves electrical appliances _____ they are fast and
                                                     2
convenient. For example, she loves her microwave _____ she can
                                                         3
use it to thaw meat quickly. She enjoys shopping for the latest kitchen devices,

_____ some of them are very expensive.
     4

   Beth has a different attitude about modern technology. She prefers not to use

electrical appliances. For instance, she never uses a microwave _____ she
                                                                      5
thinks the radiation is bad. She dries her clothes outside on a line _____
                                                                          6
she likes their smell after they've been in the fresh air. She washes her dishes by hand

_____ she says dishwashers waste energy. Pam doesn't understand why
     7
Beth is so old-fashioned. But _____ the sisters have different lifestyles,
                                     8
they appreciate and enjoy one another very much.

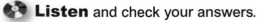 **Listen** and check your answers.

B **Talk** with a partner. Compare Mr. Speedy and Mr. Thrifty. Use *because* and *although*.

Mr. Speedy drives to work because it's fast.

Although driving is faster, Mr. Thrifty takes the subway to work because it's cheaper.

Mr. Speedy	Mr. Thrifty
drives to work	takes the subway to work
shops online	shops in stores
buys his lunch	brings lunch from home
travels by plane	travels by train
calls directory assistance for a phone number	uses the phone book
buys cakes at a bakery	bakes his own cakes

Write sentences about Mr. Speedy and Mr. Thrifty.

Mr. Speedy drives to work because it's fast.
Although driving is faster, Mr. Thrifty takes the subway to work because it's cheaper.

3 Communicate

A **Work** with a partner. Ask and answer questions about the items in Exercise 2B. Give reasons for your answers.

> **A** Do you drive to work or take the subway?
> **B** Well, although driving is faster, I take the subway.
> **A** Why?
> **B** Because I don't have a car!

Useful language

Use *neither* when both answers to a question are negative.

A Do you drive to work or take the subway?
B Neither. I ride my bike.

B **Share** information about your partner.

1 Before you read

Talk with your classmates. Answer the questions.

1. How do you stay in touch with friends and family in your native country?
2. What is a *blog*? Do you write or read one?

2 Read

SELF-STUDY
AUDIO CD

Read the blog. Listen and read again.

Search Blog   >>Next Blog>>   Sign Up! / Sign In.

Hernando's Blog

Sunday, January 20th
Today, I went with my buddy Rich to a videoconferencing center here in Chicago. It was his birthday, and by using videoconferencing, he was able to have a virtual "party" with his relatives in Guatemala. It was amazing! Rich sat in front of a wide-screen TV here. Meanwhile, his whole family was in front of a screen thousands of miles away, and he could talk to everybody together. I think videoconferencing is an innovative way to keep in touch, even though it's not very convenient. I'm going to find out more about it.

Monday, January 21st
Today, I looked online for videoconferencing centers. Most are for business, so I imagine the costs are outrageous. The center Rich used last night specializes in "reunions" between immigrants and their families in Latin America. First, you have to decide on a date and time. Then, the center here makes the arrangement with a center in the other country. It seems to be pretty popular!

Wednesday, January 23rd
I found out about the costs. The center here charges $40 for a half hour. I think that's reasonable. Luckily, the fee at this center covers the expenses in both countries, so the person in the other country doesn't have to pay anything.

Thursday, January 24th
Well, I picked a date and time for a videoconference with my parents. I want them to meet my fiancée. This is going to be great – I'll be able to see the look on their faces when they "meet" her. Can't do that with a phone or e-mail!

3 After you read

A Check your understanding.

Look at the reading tip. Then write *F* for fact or *O* for opinion, based on the reading.

> Critical readers recognize the difference between facts and opinions. Facts are known or proven. Opinions are feelings or beliefs.

_F_ 1. Videoconferences can connect people who are thousands of miles apart.

___ 2. Videoconferencing is not convenient.

___ 3. Videoconferencing centers are listed online.

___ 4. The cost of business videoconferences is probably outrageous.

___ 5. The Chicago center charges $40 for a half hour of videoconferencing.

___ 6. The cost for a half hour is reasonable.

B Build your vocabulary.

1. Read the dictionary entry. How many definitions are there?

> **virtual** /*adj*/ **1** almost a particular thing or quality **2** occurring or existing online, not as a physical reality – **virtually** /*adv*/

2. Underline the words from the chart in the reading. Use a dictionary. Write the correct definition to fit the reading. Write related words and their part of speech.

Vocabulary	Definition	Related words and part of speech
1. virtual	*occurring or existing online, not as a physical reality*	*virtually (adverb)*
2. amazing		
3. outrageous		
4. popular		
5. reasonable		
6. luckily		

C Talk with a partner.

1. Give an example of an amazing new technology.
2. What do you think is a reasonable price for a computer?
3. Do you think videoconferencing will become more popular? Why or why not?

Writing

1 Before you write

A Work in a small group. Make a list of time-saving devices you and your classmates use. Write one advantage and one disadvantage of each.

Device	Advantage	Disadvantage
electronic calculator	does math quickly	breaks easily
1.		
2.		
3.		
4.		
5.		
6.		
7.		
8.		

B Read the paragraph.

My Favorite Time-saving Device

Voice mail is my favorite time-saving device. It has several advantages. Before I had voice mail, I used to answer my phone every time it rang, even if I was busy. But with voice mail, I don't have to interrupt my work. The caller can just leave a message, and I can get it later. Another benefit of voice mail is that it allows me to avoid talking to people I don't want to talk to. But, of course, that is also a disadvantage because they can avoid talking to me! Another problem is that not only friends leave messages. Sometimes there are voice-mail messages from salespeople. So even though voice mail is very convenient, it has drawbacks as well.

One way of organizing a paragraph is by describing advantages and disadvantages.

C Work with a partner. Complete the diagram of the model paragraph.

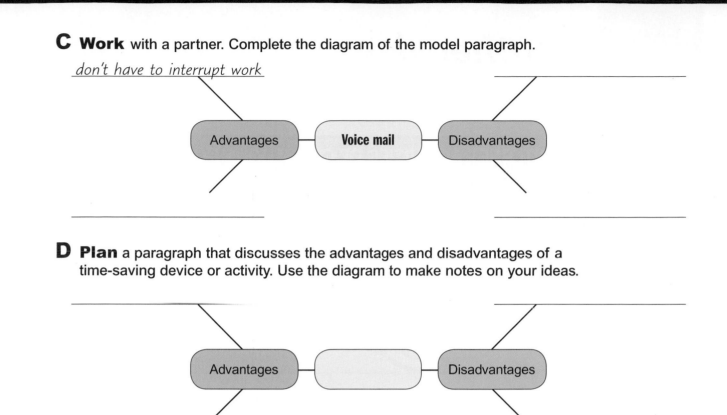

don't have to interrupt work

Advantages — **Voice mail** — Disadvantages

D Plan a paragraph that discusses the advantages and disadvantages of a time-saving device or activity. Use the diagram to make notes on your ideas.

Advantages — — Disadvantages

2 Write

Write a paragraph about the advantages and disadvantages of a time-saving device or activity. Use the paragraph in Exercise 1B and the diagrams in Exercises 1C and 1D to help you.

3 After you write

A Check your writing.

	Yes	No
1. My topic sentence names the time-saving device or activity.	☐	☐
2. I described at least two advantages and two disadvantages.	☐	☐
3. I used *because, even though,* and *although* when it was appropriate.	☐	☐

B Share your writing with a partner.

1. Take turns. Read your paragraph to a partner.
2. Comment on your partner's paragraph. Ask your partner a question about the paragraph. Tell your partner one thing you learned.

Lesson F *Another view*

1 Life-skills reading

DAILY INTERNET ACTIVITIES OF GREEN COUNTY RESIDENTS			
What activities do you do on the Internet on an average day?	**Percent of Individuals**		
	2005	**2006**	**2007**
Chat or online discussion	18	22	24
Electronic banking	14	23	30
Download music	24	18	16
Get information	30	32	35
Play games	24	26	28
Shopping	21	29	37
Send and receive e-mail	51	58	72
Watch videos on a video-sharing site	9	11	15

A Read the questions. Look at the table. Circle the answers.

1. In 2005, the most popular use of the Internet was _____ .
   a to get information
   b. to do electronic banking
   c. to send and receive e-mail
   d. none of the above

2. In 2005, fewer than 20 percent of the people in the survey used the Internet _____ .
   a. to do electronic banking
   b. to watch videos
   c. to chat
   d. all of the above

3. In 2007, getting information was less popular than _____ .
   a. shopping
   b. sending e-mail
   c. both a and b
   d. neither a nor b

4. From 2005 to 2007, there was a decline in the percentage of people who used the Internet _____ .
   a. to watch videos
   b. to download music
   c. to chat
   d. all of the above

5. From 2005 to 2007, the greatest increase was in _____ .
   a. sending and receiving e-mail
   b. chatting
   c. playing games
   d. none of the above

6. In 2006, playing games was more popular than _____ .
   a. downloading music
   b. watching videos
   c. shopping
   d. both a and b

B Talk with your classmates. Which activities in the table do you think will become more popular or less popular in the future? Why?

2 Fun with language

A **Write** the numbers 1 to 10 to show how you use the Internet. Write *1* next to the activity you do the most and *10* for the activity you do the least. Then talk with a partner. Compare your information.

What activities do you do on the Internet?			
Participate in an online discussion		Shop	
Electronic banking		Read the news	
Download music		Send and receive e-mail	
Get information		Watch videos on a video-sharing site	
Play games		Other use:	

Survey your class about the activities. What is the most common use for the Internet in your class?

B **Work** in a small group. Discuss. What are the advantages and disadvantages of the time-saving devices below? Which ones changed the world the most in your opinion? Why do you think so?

Share your ideas with your classmates.

3 Wrap up

Complete the **Self-assessment** on page 143.

Review

1 Listening

🔘 **Listen.** Take notes on a radio interview.

Characteristics of tutors	Requirements to be a tutor
1. *compassionate – care about helping*	4.
2.	5.
3.	6.

Talk with a partner. Check your answers.

2 Grammar

A Write. Complete the story.

A Love of Technology

My friend Bob loves technology. ___As soon as___ a new computer
<u>1. As soon as / Until</u>
comes out, he buys it. The same is true with his cell phone. He doesn't wait

_____ the end of the contract. _____ his cell phone is
2. as soon as / until   3. Because / Even though
still good, he buys a new one. _____ he loves the latest technology,
                               4. Because / Even though
his house is filled with new devices. _____ he has the newest devices,
                                      5. Although / Until
he keeps the old ones. His wife is unhappy. She has told him, "No more electronic

gadgets _____ you get rid of the old ones."
        6. as soon as / until

B Write. Look at the words that are underlined in the answers. Write
the questions.

1. *A* _____

   B <u>Bob</u> loves technology.

2. *A* _____

   B He buys a new cell phone <u>as soon as a new one comes out</u>.

3. *A* _____

   B His house is filled with <u>new devices</u>.

4. *A* _____

   B <u>Because of all the electronic gadgets</u>, Bob's wife is unhappy.

Talk with a partner. Ask and answer the questions.

82 Review: Units 5 & 6

3 Pronunciation: stressed and unstressed words

Content words (nouns, main verbs, adverbs, adjectives, negatives, and question words) are usually stressed. Function words (pronouns, prepositions, conjunctions, articles, *to be* verbs, and auxiliary verbs) are usually not stressed.

A 💿 **Listen** to the stressed and unstressed words in each sentence. The stressed words are underlined.

1. <u>Pam</u> <u>loves</u> <u>electrical</u> <u>appliances</u> because they <u>save</u> her <u>time</u>.
2. She <u>wants</u> to <u>volunteer</u> in the <u>health-care</u> <u>field</u>.
3. Even though <u>computers</u> are <u>time-savers</u>, <u>some</u> <u>people</u> <u>don't</u> <u>use</u> them.
4. Will he <u>go</u> to <u>sleep</u> as soon as his <u>visitors</u> <u>leave</u>?

💿 **Listen again and repeat.** Stress the underlined content words.

B 💿 **Listen and repeat.** Then underline the stressed content words.

1. She delivers meals to seniors.
2. Volunteers should be patient and compassionate.
3. Do you walk to work or drive?
4. Mr. Chung isn't a fan of e-mail.

Read your sentences to a partner. Compare your answers.

C Read the paragraph. Underline the stressed words.

Ingrid worked with computers in her native country, so that's the job she wants here. She's been looking for several months, but she hasn't found one yet. Finally, she decided to do some volunteer work until she could find a paying job. Ingrid volunteers at the local zoo. She does office work on the computer.

Talk with a partner. Compare your answers. Read the paragraph to your partner.

D Write four sentences from Units 5 and 6. Then work with a partner. Underline the stressed words in your partner's sentences.

1. _____
2. _____
3. _____
4. _____

1 Talk about the pictures

A What do you see?

B What is happening?

Shopping

CAMERA SALE

BEST DEALS

PHOTO PRO

GOOD BUYS

Customer Service

Store Return Policy:

CHECKOUT

Rosa

Store Return Policy:

2 Listening

SELF-STUDY
AUDIO CD **A** 🔊 **Listen** and answer the questions.

    1. Who are the speakers?

    2. What are they talking about?

SELF-STUDY
AUDIO CD **B** 🔊 **Listen again.** Complete the chart.

1. kind of camera Rosa bought	*a digital camera*
2. problem	
3. date purchased	
4. today's date	
5. store policy for refunds	
6. store policy for exchanges	

Listen again. Check your answers.

SELF-STUDY
AUDIO CD **C** 🔊 **Read.** Complete the story. Listen and check your answers.

condition	defective	merchandise	store credit
customer service	exchanges	refund	warranty

        Rosa wants to return the camera that she bought and get a _____*refund*_____ .
1

She is told that she needs to speak with someone in _____ . The clerk
2

there asks Rosa if the camera is _____ . Rosa says that it's not broken, but
3

she doesn't like the screen. The clerk tells her about the store policy for returns and

_____ . It's too late for Rosa to return the camera, but she can exchange
4

it if the _____ is in perfect _____ . Rosa still has the camera
5   **6**

box with the instruction book and the _____ card. Since Rosa is in a hurry,
7

she decides to get a _____ , and she will use it at a later time.
8

D Discuss. Talk with your classmates.

    1. What are some reasons that people may want to return merchandise to a store?

    2. What are some situations where it may be impossible to return merchandise?

    3. Do you think it is right for people to get their money back for something
       that they have used? Why or why not?

Adjective clauses

1 Grammar focus: *who* and *that* as the subject of a dependent clause

Simple sentences	Sentences with an adjective clause
The camera costs only $99. It is on sale.	The camera that is on sale costs only $99.
The manager helped the customer. She lost her receipt.	The manager helped the customer who lost her receipt.

For a grammar explanation, turn to page 150.

2 Practice

Useful language
Adjective clauses that describe people may begin with *that* or *who*.

A Write. Combine the sentences. Change the second sentence into an adjective clause with *that* or *who*.

1. I want to buy a camera. It's not too expensive.
   I want to buy a camera that's not too expensive.

2. I'd like to get a good camera. It will last for many years.
   _____

3. Many people shop online. They are looking for cameras.
   _____

4. My friend told me about a camera store. It sells used merchandise.
   _____

5. Customers like to shop at Super Camera. They appreciate good service.
   _____

6. The clerk is very helpful. He works in customer service.
   _____

7. These days, most people want a digital camera. It holds a lot of pictures.
   _____

8. Digital cameras are sometimes difficult to use. They have small screens.
   _____

🔊 **Listen** and check your answers.

B Talk with a partner. Ask and answer questions to identify the following people in the picture: the cashier, the cleaning person, the customer, the greeter, the stock clerk, and the store manager. Use adjective clauses with *who* or *that*. Choose verbs from the box.

clean	have	listen	smile	sweep
give	hold	put	stand	wear

> *A* Which one is the cashier?
> *B* He's the man who's putting the video camera into the bag.
>
> *A* You mean the one who's smiling?
> *B* Right.

Write sentences about the people in the picture.

The cashier is the man who's putting the video camera into the bag.

3 Communicate

A Work in a small group. Ask and answer questions about the topics. Use adjective clauses.

- supermarkets
- restaurants
- salesclerks
- clothing stores
- malls
- (your idea)

> *A* Nadia, what kind of supermarkets do you like?
> *B* I like supermarkets that are open 24 hours a day. What about you, Phuong?
> *C* I like supermarkets that have lots of fresh fish.

B Share information about your classmates.

Lesson C Adjective clauses

1 Grammar focus: *that* as the object of a dependent clause

Simple sentences	Sentences with an adjective clause
I like the car. You bought it.	I like the car (that) you bought.
The mechanic has 20 years of experience. I use him.	The mechanic (that) I use has 20 years of experience.

For a grammar explanation, turn to page 150.

2 Practice

A Write. Combine the sentences. Change the second sentence into an adjective clause with *that*.

1. Suzy is a good friend. I've known her for several years.
   Suzy is a good friend that I've known for several years.

2. Last January, her old car stopped working. She was driving it.
   _____

3. The mechanic couldn't fix it. Her friend recommended the mechanic.
   _____

4. Finally, she decided to buy a used car from a man. She knew the man at work.
   _____

5. He's an honest person. She trusts him completely.
   _____

6. He gave her a good price. She couldn't refuse it.
   _____

7. The used car is only three years old. He sold her the car.
   _____

8. It's a reliable car. She can drive it for a long time.
   _____

🔵 **Listen** and check your answers.

> **Useful language**
> You can omit the word *that* when it is the object of the dependent clause.

B Talk with a partner. Ted and Lisa got married recently. Unfortunately, they have had some bad luck. Look at the chart and make sentences by choosing an item from each column.

> The dishes that Ted and Lisa received from Aunt May were broken.

computer	found on the Internet	the wrong size
dishes	bought on sale	scratched
car	ordered from a catalog	broken
camera	got as a wedding present	damaged
rug	received from Aunt May	torn
lamps	picked up at a garage sale	the wrong color
coffee table	purchased from a friend	too slow

Write sentences about Ted and Lisa.

The dishes that they received from Aunt May were broken.

3 Communicate

A Work in a small group. Tell about a shopping "mistake." Include the information below.

- What was the item?
- When did you buy it?
- Where did you buy it?
- What was wrong with it?
- What did you do about it?

> **A** The chicken that I bought last week at Paglia's Meats was spoiled.
> **B** What did you do about it?
> **A** I took it back to the store and asked them to give me a fresh package.

Useful language
Use the following adjectives to say what is wrong with something you bought: *broken, defective, damaged, spoiled, torn, too big, too small.*

B Share information about your classmates.

1 Before you read

Talk with your classmates. Answer the questions.

1. Have you ever tried to exchange an item or get a refund? Tell about your experience.
2. In your native country, is it easy or difficult for people to get a refund for something that they purchased?

2 Read

SELF-STUDY
AUDIO CD

Read the newspaper advice column. Listen and read again.

Dear Smart Shopper,

I'm a jewelry lover, and I enjoy shopping online. Unfortunately, I just bought a pair of gold earrings that I don't like. When I tried to return them, I learned that the seller has a no-return policy. Don't I have the right to get a refund?

Mad Madelyn

Dear Mad Madelyn,

If the merchandise is defective, the seller must return your money or make an exchange. However, if the merchandise was in good condition when you received it, and if the retailer has a no-return policy, there is nothing you can do. This is true for store purchases as well as Internet purchases. In the future, here are some questions you should ask before you buy anything:

- Does the seller say "satisfaction guaranteed or your money back"?
- Is there a time limit on returns, such as two weeks?
- Who pays the shipping costs on items that are returned?
- Do you need to return the merchandise in its original package?
- Is the original receipt required?
- Does the retailer give a store credit instead of a cash refund?
- If the retailer has a store in your area, can you return the merchandise to the store instead of shipping it?

Next time, find the return policy on the merchant's Web site and print it, or ask the merchant for the return policy in writing. It's important to get all the facts that you need before you buy!

Smart Shopper

Sometimes an important word is replaced by a synonym. This makes the reading more interesting. For example, *seller* and *retailer* are two nouns that have the same meaning.

3 After you read

A Check your understanding.

1. What is Madelyn's problem?
2. If an item is defective, does a purchaser have the right to return it?
3. Does Madelyn have the right to get a refund? Why or why not?
4. Is the Smart Shopper's advice for Internet purchases, store purchases, or both?
5. What should Madelyn have done before she bought the earrings?
6. What is the meaning of "satisfaction guaranteed or your money back"?
7. *Seller* and *retailer* are synonyms. What is another word in the reading with the same meaning?
8. Smart Shopper lists several questions that purchasers should ask before they buy. In your opinion, which question is the most important?

B Build your vocabulary.

Compound nouns are *noun* + *noun* combinations that have special meanings. Sometimes you can explain compound nouns with adjective clauses. For example, a *jewelry lover* is a person who loves jewelry.

1. Find compound nouns in the reading that match the explanations. Write them in the chart.

Compound noun	Explanation
1. *jewelry lover*	a person who loves jewelry
2.	a limit that is related to time
3.	costs that are related to shipping
4.	a credit that is given by a store
5.	a refund that is made in cash
6.	a policy that is related to returns
7.	
8.	

2. Find two more compound nouns in the reading. Write them in the chart. Use adjective clauses to explain what they mean.

3. Work in a small group. Make a list of other compound nouns you know. Use adjective clauses to explain what they mean.

C Talk with a partner.

1. Are you a jewelry lover? What do you love to buy?
2. What things have a time limit?
3. Have you ever gotten a cash refund? What for?

Lesson E *Writing*

1 Before you write

A Talk with a partner. List some reasons why people should or shouldn't shop online.

Why people should shop online	Why people shouldn't shop online
It's convenient.	It's hard to choose merchandise you can't touch.

B Read the paragraph.

Why You Shouldn't Shop Online

There are some good reasons why you shouldn't shop online. First, it's hard to choose merchandise that you can't touch. For example, a piece of jewelry might look very good on the computer screen, but after you buy it and look at it closely, you may find that it's very ugly and poorly made. Furthermore, shopping online is slow. It may take several days to receive the merchandise. If you are not satisfied, it may take weeks to exchange the merchandise or get your money back. Finally, shopping online can be dangerous. People can steal your credit card number and use it to buy expensive items. An irresponsible seller can take your money and never send you the merchandise. I'm going to do my shopping in stores!

> Use transition words such as *first, second, next, furthermore, moreover,* and *finally* to signal a list of reasons in a paragraph.

C Complete the outline with information from the model paragraph.

Transition words	Reasons and supporting details
First	First reason: *Hard to choose merchandise you can't touch.*
	Example: _____
_____	Second reason: _____
	Fact: _____
	Fact: _____
_____	Third reason: _____
	Fact: _____
	Fact: _____

D Plan a paragraph about why you *should* shop online. Think of two or more reasons and one or more supporting details (facts or examples) for each reason. Make notes on your ideas in an outline like the one in Exercise 1C. Use your own paper.

2 Write

Write a paragraph about why you *should* shop online. Use the paragraph in Exercise 1B and the outlines in Exercises 1C and 1D to help you.

3 After you write

A Check your writing.

	Yes	No
1. I wrote two or more reasons to shop online.	☐	☐
2. I gave one or more supporting details (facts or examples) for each reason.	☐	☐
3. I used transition words like *first*, *furthermore*, and *finally* to signal my list of reasons.	☐	☐

B Share your writing with a partner.

1. Take turns. Read your paragraph to a partner.
2. Comment on your partner's paragraph. Ask your partner a question about the paragraph. Tell your partner one thing you learned.

Another view

1 Life-skills reading

JedsSports.com

RETURNED-MERCHANDISE FORM

Please complete this form and send it with the returned merchandise within 21 days to JedsSports.com, 887 13th Avenue, San Francisco, CA 94122. Include a copy of the invoice and the original packaging. Call us for a Returned-Merchandise Authorization number (M–F, 8 a.m.–5 p.m., PST) at 800-555-4143.

Name: *Rita Miller*   **RMA#:** *98704370*   **Check one:**

Address	*271 Dade Drive*	City	*Largo*	State	*FL*	Zip	*33771*	☐ **Store Credit**

List items for return: ☑ **Exchange**

Item #	Description	Size	Color	Reason	Additional Comments:
P4103	*sweatshirt*	*medium*	*red*	*wrong size*	*I ordered a large.*

List items to receive in exchange:

Item #	Description	Size	Color		
P4128	*sweatshirt*	*large*	*red*		

A Read the questions. Look at the returned-merchandise form. Circle the answers.

1. Why is the buyer using this form?
   a. She wants her money back.
   b. She wants a store credit.
   c. She wants to exchange the merchandise.
   d. none of the above

2. What does the buyer need to include with this form?
   a. the invoice
   b. the item that she is returning
   c. the original packaging
   d. all of the above

3. Which statement is true?
   a. The buyer must return the items within 21 days.
   b. The buyer is satisfied with her purchase.
   c. The buyer needs a smaller sweatshirt.
   d. The buyer lives in California.

4. Which statement is *not* true?
   a. The buyer is returning one item.
   b. The buyer needs a different size.
   c. The merchandise was defective.
   d. The buyer wants the same color.

5. What does "RMA#" mean?
   a. returned-merchandise invoice number
   b. returned-merchandise authorization number
   c. credit card number
   d. none of the above

6. How did Rita get the RMA number?
   a. She e-mailed the store.
   b. She called an 800 number.
   c. She got it from the original invoice.
   d. It was written on the merchandise.

B Talk with your classmates. Do you think it is difficult to return or exchange merchandise at this store. Why or why not?

2 Fun with language

A Work with a partner. Match the idioms with the definitions. Then write new sentences using the idioms.

Idiom

1. This dress is **a steal**! Yesterday, I saw it for $30 more in another store. __e__

2. You paid $299 for a camera phone? What **a rip-off**! ____

3. My shoes **cost a fortune**, but they look beautiful and fit perfectly. I love them! ____

4. These CDs are **marked down** from their regular price. ____

5. Stella is going to **shop around** for her husband's birthday present. ____

6. Jack bought a used car, and it turned out to be a real **lemon**. ____

Definition

a. reduced in price

b. look in more than one store

c. something that costs much more than it's worth

d. something that is poorly made

e. something that is a really good price

f. are very expensive

B Work with a partner. Role-play one of the following situations. Write a short conversation and act it out in front of the class.

1. You want to return a textbook to the school bookstore. You bought the book three weeks ago. Since you bought it, you have changed your class and you no longer need the book.

> *A* I'd like to return this textbook.
> *B* What's the problem?
> *A* I changed my class, and I don't need it any longer.
> *B* Do you have the receipt?
> *A* No. I lost it, but you can see that the book is new.
> *B* I'm sorry, but you'll need to show us the receipt.

2. You bought some milk at the supermarket. When you get home, you find that it is sour. The expiration date on the milk carton was two weeks ago. You are annoyed, and you take the milk back to the store.

3. For your birthday, you received a nice sweater that was purchased at an expensive shop in the mall. The sweater is too small, and it's a color that you don't like. You want to exchange the sweater for something else, but you don't have the receipt.

Perform your role play for the class.

3 Wrap up

Complete the **Self-assessment** on page 144.

Lesson A *Get ready*

1 Talk about the pictures

A What do you see?

B What is happening?

2 Listening

SELF-STUDY
AUDIO CD **A** 🔊 **Listen** and answer the questions.

    1. Who are the speakers?

    2. What are they talking about?

SELF-STUDY
AUDIO CD **B** 🔊 **Listen again.** Complete the diagram.

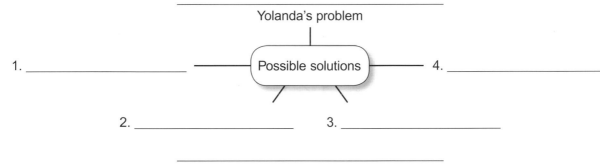

Yolanda's problem

1. _____ — (Possible solutions) — 4. _____

2. _____   3. _____

Yolanda's decision

Listen again. Check your answers.

SELF-STUDY
AUDIO CD **C** 🔊 **Read.** Complete the story. Listen and check your answers.

chart	deal with	initials	share
close up	exhausted	negotiate	work (something) out

    Yolanda and David work at Daria's Donut Shop. Lately, David has been leaving work early, and Yolanda has to ___close up___ the shop by herself. Tonight, Yolanda
          1
is having coffee with her friends. She is _____ . Her friends give her
                        2
advice. Teresa thinks she should talk to her boss, but Yolanda wants to try to
_____ things _____ with David first. Julie thinks Yolanda should
          3
make a _____ of their duties. Then she should _____ with David and
          4   5
decide who is going to do which tasks. When they finish a task, they should write
their _____ on the chart. If David isn't doing his _____ of the work,
          6   7
it will show in the chart. Then Yolanda can show the chart to their boss and let her
_____ the situation.
    8

D **Discuss.** Talk with your classmates. Have you ever had a problem at work or school? How did you solve it?

Tense contrast

1 Grammar focus: present perfect and present perfect continuous

Present perfect (recently finished action)	**Present perfect continuous (continuing action)**
Yolanda has (just) mopped the floor. It's clean now.	Yolanda has been mopping the floor for 15 minutes.

For a grammar explanation, turn to page 151.
For a list of past participles, turn to page 154.

2 Practice

A Write. Complete the sentences. Use the present perfect or present perfect continuous forms of the verbs. Use *just* where possible.

1. Daria Thompson is the owner of Daria's Donut Shop.

   She ___*has been selling*___ donuts at this location for
   (sell)
   more than 20 years.

2. It's 7:00 a.m. Daria _____ donuts for
   (make)
   three hours.

3. It's 7:30 a.m. Daria _____ the shop
   (open)
   for customers.

4. It's 10:30 a.m. Daria's son _____ her
   (help)
   all morning.

5. He _____ cleaning the counters and
   (finish)
   shelves. Everything is spotless.

6. Daria needs more help in the shop. She _____
   (interview)
   candidates all week.

7. Yolanda's shift begins at 6:00 a.m. today. She _____ for
   (wait)
   the bus for 30 minutes. She's worried that she's going to be late.

8. It's 6:05 a.m. Yolanda _____ to say she will be late.
   (call)

Listen and check your answers.

B Talk with a partner. Look at Yolanda's work schedule. Make sentences about the things she has just done and has been doing at the following times: 6:15, 6:30, 7:30, 11:00, 12:00, 2:00, and 4:00.

> It's 6:15 a.m. Yolanda has just arrived.

> It's 11:00 a.m. Yolanda has been serving customers for three and a half hours.

Yolanda's Schedule

6:15 a.m.	Arrive Turn off the security alarm
6:30 a.m.	Open the cash register Make coffee
7:30 a.m.	Open the shop for customers
7:30 a.m.–11:00 a.m.	Serve customers Take phone orders
11:00 a.m.–12:00 noon	Eat lunch Go to the bank
12:00 noon–4:00 p.m.	Serve customers Take phone orders
2:00 p.m.	Refill sugar containers Receive shipment of coffee
4:00 p.m.	Go home

Write sentences about Yolanda's schedule.

It's 6:15 a.m. Yolanda has just arrived.
It's 11:00 a.m. Yolanda has been serving customers for three and a half hours.

3 Communicate

A Work with a partner. Think about your own schedule. Your partner says a time. You say what you have been doing and what you have just done.

> *A* Natalia, it's 10:30 a.m.
> *B* I've been working for two hours.
>   I've just read my e-mail.

B Share information about your partner.

> It's 10:30 a.m. Natalia has been working for two hours. She has just read her e-mail.

Lesson C *Participial adjectives*

1 Grammar focus: adjectives ending in *-ed* and *-ing*

Adjective *-ed*	Adjective *-ing*	
I'm tired of this job. He's interested in this task.	This is a tiring job. This is an interesting task.	This job is tiring. This task is interesting.

For a grammar explanation, turn to page 151.

2 Practice

A Write. Circle the correct adjective.

1. **A** I heard that Juan and his friends went to a party after work. How was the party?
   B It was really (exciting) / excited.

2. **A** How did Juan feel the next day at work?
   B He was **exhausting** / **exhausted**.

3. **A** How long did he have to work?
   B He had to work from 9:30 to 6:30. It was a **tiring** / **tired** day.

4. **A** Does Juan usually start working at 9:30?
   B No, he overslept! He was **shocking** / **shocked** that he didn't hear the alarm clock.

5. **A** How did his boss react when he showed up late?
   B His boss was **irritating** / **irritated**.

6. **A** What did his boss say to him?
   B He told Juan that he was **disappointing** / **disappointed** in him.

7. **A** Juan didn't have a good day, I guess. What did he do later that night?
   B He stayed home and had a **relaxing** / **relaxed** night in front of the TV.

8. **A** So, is Juan going to go out again on a weeknight?
   B I don't think so. He said it was an **exhausting** / **exhausted** experience.

🔊 **Listen** and check your answers. Then practice with a partner.

B Talk with a partner. For each picture, describe the person and the activity. Choose participial adjectives from the boxes.

The man is excited. Getting an award is exciting.

Positive	
amusing	amused
exciting	excited
interesting	interested

Negative	
boring	bored
frightening	frightened
frustrating	frustrated

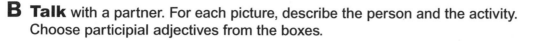

Write two sentences about each picture.

The man is excited.
Getting an award is exciting.

3 Communicate

A Work in a small group. Ask and answer questions about your experiences. Use the adjectives from Exercise 2B.

> A What's an amusing experience that you have had at work?
> B I was very amused when . . . . It was amusing because . . .

B Share information about your classmates.

1 Before you read

Talk with your classmates. Answer the questions.

1. What are some skills, such as following directions, that are necessary for most jobs?
2. What special skills do you have?

2 Read

SELF-STUDY AUDIO CD **Read** the magazine article. Listen and read again.

Hard and Soft Job Skills

Som Sarawong has been working as an automotive technician at George's Auto Repair for over five years. Today was a special day for Som, a 35-year-old Thai immigrant, because he received the Employee of the Year award. According to Ed Overton, Som's boss, Som received the award "because he's a great 'people person' and he has superb technical skills. I even have him work on my own car!"

Som has the two kinds of skills that are necessary to be successful and move up in his career: soft skills and hard skills. Soft skills are personal and social skills. Som gets along with his co-workers. He has a strong work ethic; in five years, he has never been late or absent from work. Customers trust him. Hard skills, on the other hand, are the technical skills a person needs to do a job. Som can repair cars, trucks, and motorcycles. He learned from his father, who was also a mechanic. Then he took classes and got a certificate as an auto technician.

Soft and hard skills are equally important, but hard skills are easier to teach and assess than soft skills. People can learn how to use a machine and then take a test on their knowledge. However, it's harder to teach people how to be cooperative and have a good work ethic. George Griffith, the owner of George's Auto Repair, explains, "I've been working in this business for over 30 years, and most of the time when I've needed to fire someone, it was because of weak people skills, not because they didn't have technical abilities." Soft skills and good technical knowledge are a winning combination, and today, Som Sarawong was the winner.

> Quotations are used to explain or support a main idea. They also make a reading more interesting.

3 After you read

A Check your understanding.

1. According to Som Sarawong's boss, why did Som get the Employee of the Year award?
2. What's the difference between a soft skill and a hard skill? Give examples.
3. Which example shows that Som has a good work ethic?
4. Why is it easier to teach hard skills than soft skills?
5. According to what George Griffith says, do more workers lose their jobs because of weak soft skills or weak hard skills?
6. Do you agree with George Griffith? Why or why not?

> **Culture note**
> The expression "work ethic" is the belief that if you work hard in life you will get ahead and become successful.

B Build your vocabulary.

1. Find an example in the reading of each prefix and root. Write it in the chart.

2. Use a dictionary. Write the meaning of the words.

3. Guess the meaning of the prefixes and roots in the chart.

Prefixes and roots	Example from reading	Meaning of word	Meaning of prefix or root
1. re-	repair	to fix what is torn or broken	again
2. co-			
3. auto			
4. tech			
5. super			
6. mot			
7. equ			

4. Work in a small group. Make a list of other words you know with the same prefixes and roots. Write a sentence for each new word.

C Talk with a partner.

1. What is something that you can do superbly?
2. What are some examples of technical skills?
3. What is a hobby or profession that requires good technical skills?
4. Are you good at repairing things? What can you repair?

1 Before you write

A Talk with a partner. Answer the questions.

1. What is a cover letter? What information does it include?
2. Have you ever written a cover letter? Tell about your experience.

B Read the cover letter.

> Ester Yitbarek
> 4 South 8th Ave., Apt. 303
> Chicago, IL 60601
> September 30, 2008
>
> Lynn Stevens
> Director of Human Resources
> Highland School District
> 625 S. 30th St.
> Chicago, IL 60609
>
> Dear Ms. Stevens:
>
> I read your advertisement online for a position as a teacher's assistant. I am very interested in this position and have enclosed my resume.
>
> I have been working as a teacher's assistant at Hilltop Elementary School for three years. In this job, I have taught reading and math to students in small groups. I have also tutored individual students who were having problems with the lessons. I'm very interested in child development, and I love working with children. I get along very well with my co-workers, and I'm also skilled at dealing with parents.
>
> I am planning to move to a new home in your district. I hope you will call me to schedule an interview. I look forward to hearing from you.
>
> Sincerely,
>
> *Ester Yitbarek*
>
> Ester Yitbarek

Culture note
Applicants are always expected to include a resume – a written statement of their educational and work experience – with their cover letter.

C Work with a partner. Answer the questions.

1. Who wrote the letter?
2. Who did she write it to?
3. What position is she applying for?
4. Where did she hear about the job?
5. How much experience does she have?
6. What are some of her skills?

> In the body of a cover letter, include:
> - the title of the job you are applying for
> - how you found out about the job
> - information about your skills and experience

D Plan a cover letter for a real or an imaginary job. Complete the information.

1. Date: _____

2. Inside address

   Name and title of addressee: _____

   Address: _____

3. Position you are applying for

   Job title: _____

   How you found out about it: _____

4. Your skills and experience: _____

   _____

   _____

   _____

2 Write

Write a cover letter for a real or an imaginary job that you are interested in. Use the cover letter in Exercise 1B and your outline in Exercise 1D to help you.

3 After you write

A Check your writing.

	Yes	No
1. My first sentence says the title of the job I am applying for.	☐	☐
2. I included how I heard about the job.	☐	☐
3. I gave two or more examples of my skills and experience.	☐	☐

B Share your writing with a partner.

1. Take turns. Read your letter to a partner.
2. Comment on your partner's letter. Ask your partner a question about the letter. Tell your partner one thing you learned.

Another view

1 Life-skills reading

Skills Required in the Fastest-growing Service Occupations

Skills	Janitor	Waiter	Food-service worker	Home health aide	Nursing aide
Listening well / Understanding instructions	●	●	●	●	●
Managing time	●	●			●
Monitoring one's own performance and that of others				●	●
Reading comprehension related to work documents	●	●		●	●
Talking to others to convey information effectively	●	●	●	●	●
Teaching job duties to others	●	●	●	●	●

Source: www7.nationalacademies.org/CFE/future_Skill_Demands_Mary_Gatta_Paper.pdf

A Read the questions. Look at the chart. Circle the answers.

1. Which occupation requires listening?
   a. food-service worker
   b. janitor
   c. nursing aide
   d. all of the above

2. Which skill is required by all of the occupations?
   a. reading comprehension
   b. monitoring performance
   c. teaching others
   d. none of the above

3. Which skill is required for a food-service worker?
   a. monitoring performance
   b. listening well
   c. reading
   d. managing time

4. Which skills are required for a waiter?
   a. listening well
   b. managing time
   c. reading
   d. all of the above

5. Which skill is required by the fewest occupations?
   a. managing time
   b. reading comprehension
   c. monitoring performance
   d. teaching others

6. Which occupation requires managing time?
   a. nursing aide
   b. home health aide
   c. food-service worker
   d. all of the above

B Talk with your classmates. Which skills from the chart do you have? Which skills have you used at a previous or current job?

2 Fun with language

A Work in a small group. Read about the four people who are applying for a manager position at the Custom Cleaning Company. Discuss each person. Then make a group decision about who to hire as manager. Consider their hard and soft skills in making your decision.

Richard
- Always looks for ways to help people
- Good at teaching job duties to others
- Knows how to use the equipment
- Sometimes leaves early or arrives late for work
- Goes to night school to get a business degree

Jackie
- Manages her time well
- Good listener and communicator
- Bilingual English / Spanish
- Sometimes forgets safety rules
- Was assistant manager for five years at her previous job

Pearl
- Works well with the team
- Good listener and communicator
- Often absent from work on Fridays
- Solves problems as they happen
- 15 years' experience with the company

Hassan
- Has a positive attitude – polite and friendly
- Reads and follows instructions well
- Sometimes talks too much and doesn't finish work
- Writes reports effectively
- Bilingual English / Persian

B Share your decision with your classmates. Give reasons for your group's choice.

3 Wrap up

Complete the **Self-assessment** on page 144.

Review

1 Listening

Listen. Take notes on a class lecture.

Job skills for an electronics store	Job skills for a restaurant
1. *good communication skills*	4.
2.	5.
3.	6.

Talk with a partner. Check your answers.

2 Grammar

A Write. Complete the story.

Joanie's Problem

Joanie is at the electronics store. She wants to return a scanner. She

_____*has been talking*_____ with a clerk in customer service for the past
1. has talked / has been talking

15 minutes. He told her she could exchange the scanner. However, Joanie

_____ at scanners for several months, and she still
2. has looked / has been looking

_____ another one she likes. She wants a refund. The
3. hasn't found / hasn't been finding

clerk _____ his manager this minute to see if Joanie
4. has just called / has been calling

can get a refund, but the manager is not in his office. This situation is very

_____ for Joanie. She's _____ and wants
5. frustrating / frustrated   6. tiring / tired

to go home.

B Write. Look at the words that are underlined in the answers. Write the questions.

1. **A** _____

   B Joanie wants to return <u>her scanner</u>.

2. **A** _____

   B Joanie has been talking to the clerk <u>for 15 minutes</u>.

3. **A** _____

   B <u>The customer-service clerk</u> says that she can exchange the scanner.

Talk with a partner. Ask and answer the questions.

3 Pronunciation: stressing function words

Normally, function words such as pronouns, prepositions, conjunctions, articles, *to be* verbs, and auxiliary verbs are *not* stressed. However, when strong feelings or disagreements are expressed, function words can receive strong stress.

A **Listen** to the stressed function words in each conversation.

1. **A** Is the camera defective?
   B It's defective <u>and</u> too small!

2. **A** Don't you usually finish at 5:00?
   B I <u>do</u> usually finish at 5:00, but not today.

3. **A** Why aren't you applying for that job?
   B I <u>am</u>. I'll go there tomorrow.

4. **A** I don't trust the man who sold you this car.
   B Well, <u>I</u> <u>do</u>! It's <u>my</u> decision, not <u>yours</u>.

5. **A** Is he excited about his new job?
   B No, but his wife <u>is</u>.

6. **A** Did you put the returned merchandise on my desk?
   B No, I put it <u>in</u> your desk.

Listen again and repeat. Stress the underlined function words.

B **Listen and repeat.** Then underline the stressed function words.

1. **A** I'd like to exchange this sweater.
   B Why?
   A It's too big, and it has a hole.

2. **A** You can't leave early again!
   B Yes, I can and I will.

3. **A** Why don't you clean the counters?
   B Why don't you?

4. **A** Let's talk about a raise after you've worked here for six months.
   B Can we talk before six months?

Talk with a partner. Compare your answers.

C **Talk** with a partner. Practice the conversations. Pay attention to the stressed function words.

1. **A** We don't give refunds or exchanges on watches.
   B My warranty says you <u>can</u> if the merchandise is defective.
   A So, <u>is</u> it defective?
   B Yes, it <u>is</u>.
   A Then I <u>can</u> give you a refund.

2. **A** Who just mopped the floors, <u>you</u> or <u>Kevin</u>?
   B <u>I</u> did. <u>And</u> I cleaned the tables.
   A Good work. I <u>do</u> enjoy seeing a clean bakery.
   B And <u>I</u> love working here.

D **Write** two new conversations using stressed function words. Practice with a partner.

A Does Karen need more help?
B No, but <u>I</u> do.

1 Talk about the pictures

A What do you see?
B What is happening?

Mei

2 Listening

SELF-STUDY AUDIO CD **A** 🔊 **Listen** and answer the questions.

1. Who are the speakers?
2. What are they talking about?

SELF-STUDY AUDIO CD **B** 🔊 **Listen again.** Complete the chart.

Ideas for living green	Will the family try?
1. *walk, bike, carpool, take public transportation*	*No*
2.	
3.	
4.	
5.	
6.	

Listen again. Check your answers.

SELF-STUDY AUDIO CD **C** 🔊 **Read.** Complete the story. Listen and check your answers.

appliances	cut down on	environment	recycle
carpool	energy-efficient	global warming	responsibility

Mei was late to dinner because she was looking at the Web site of the Living Green Council. "Living green" means taking ____*responsibility*____ for saving the earth from _____2_____ . Mei tells her parents about the guest speaker who came to her class. The speaker suggested simple things people could do to reduce their energy use and protect the _____3_____ . For example, they could _____4_____ instead of driving alone, _____5_____ their bottles and cans, and use _____6_____ lightbulbs. Mei's parents agree that it is important to _____7_____ energy use since it would also help them save money. However, they can't afford to buy new _____8_____ right now.

D **Discuss.** Talk with your classmates. Which of the speaker's suggestions can you try? Which are difficult for you? Why?

Conditional sentences

1 Grammar focus: present unreal conditional

If everybody drove smaller cars, we would use less gasoline.
We would use less gasoline if everybody drove smaller cars.

For a grammar explanation, turn to page 152.

Useful language
Use *would* when you are 100 percent sure.
Use *could* if you are less certain.

2 Practice

A Write. Complete the sentences. Use the present unreal conditional.

1. Many people put their newspapers in the trash can.

   If everybody _____*recycled*_____ newspapers,
   (recycle)

   we _____*would save*_____ millions of trees.
   (save)

2. Noah never takes his car in for a tune-up.

   Noah's car _____ less gas if he
   (use)

   _____ his car regularly.
   (tune up)

3. Mr. Brown drives his own car to his job downtown.

   Mr. Brown _____ money on gas if he
   (save)

   _____ to work.
   (carpool)

4. Many items in the supermarket are packaged in plastic.

   If you _____ products that are packaged with recycled
   (buy)

   paper, you _____ to reduce global warming.
   (help)

5. Jessica always stays in the shower for a very long time.

   If Jessica _____ shorter showers, she
   (take)

   _____ water.
   (save)

6. Some kinds of fish contain large amounts of lead, a poisonous metal.

   You _____ healthier if you _____
   (be)   (stop)

   eating fish that contains lead.

   Listen and check your answers.

B Talk with a partner. Match each action with a result. Some items have more than one correct answer. Use the present unreal conditional.

> If everybody bought energy-efficient appliances, we would save electricity.

Actions	Results
buy energy-efficient appliances	save gas
fix water leaks	cut down on energy use
replace lightbulbs with energy-efficient ones	save water
recycle cans, bottles, glass, and paper	reduce air-conditioning and heating use
put enough air in their tires	reduce the amount of trash in landfills
close off unused rooms	save electricity

Write sentences about the actions and results.

If everybody bought energy-efficient appliances, we would save electricity.

3 Communicate

A Work in a small group. Look at the picture. Talk about actions people could take to help the environment at the beach.

> If people picked up the trash on the beach, everyone could enjoy a clean beach.

B Share ideas with your classmates.

Connectors

1 Grammar focus: *since, due to, consequently, as a result*

> ### Connectors of cause
> Since the earth is getting warmer, the polar ice caps are melting.
> Due to the warmer temperatures, the polar ice caps are melting.
>
> ### Connectors of effect
> The earth is getting warmer. Consequently, the polar ice caps are melting.
> The earth is getting warmer. As a result, the polar ice caps are melting.
>
> *For a grammar explanation, turn to page 152.*

> ### Useful language
> *Because* can replace *since.*
> *Because of* can replace *due to.*
> *Therefore* can replace *consequently* or *as a result.*

2 Practice

A **Write.** Combine the sentences. Use the connectors in parentheses.

1. There is a buildup of harmful gases in the atmosphere. Global warming is increasing.

   (Due to) *Due to a buildup of harmful gases in the atmosphere, global*
   warming is increasing.

2. Warm water is expanding in the oceans. The sea level is rising.

   (As a result) *Warm water is expanding in the oceans. As a result, the sea*
   level is rising.

3. The sea level is rising. Towns near oceans are in danger of flooding.

   (Since) _____

4. Global warming changes weather patterns. Many places will have less rainfall.

   (Since) _____

5. Mosquitoes will increase. There will be an increase in diseases like malaria.

   (Consequently) _____

6. Ocean water is getting warmer. Typhoons and hurricanes are becoming more frequent.

   (Due to) _____

7. Cities are growing. Many plants and animals may lose their natural habitats.

   (As a result) _____

   Listen and check your answers.

B Talk with a partner. Combine sentences in different ways using the connectors *since*, *because*, *because of*, *due to*, *consequently*, *therefore*, and *as a result*.

> **A** Since people are building homes in forests, animals are losing their natural habitats.
> **B** People are building homes in forests. As a result, animals are losing their natural habitats.

Causes	Effects
1. People are building homes in forests.	Animals are losing their natural habitats.
2. There is habitat loss.	Animals are moving into towns and cities.
3. Animals are moving into towns and cities.	The animals are frightened.
4. The animals are frightened.	Sometimes they attack people.
5. Wild animals sometimes attack people.	People are afraid of them.
6. People are afraid of wild animals.	They kill the animals.

Write sentences about the causes and effects.

Since people are building homes in forests, animals are losing their natural habitats.

3 Communicate

A Work in a small group. Read the newspaper headlines. Discuss the possible causes and effects of each event. Think of other possible headlines to discuss.

> Coyotes are losing their natural habitats. As a result, they're moving into towns.

THE MESSENGER
Another Coyote Moves into Town

THE NEWS
WHALE WASHES UP ON SHORE

THE DAILY
POLAR BEARS DROWNING AS ICE CAPS MELT

B Share information with your classmates.

1 Before you read

Talk with your classmates. Answer the questions.

1. What is a *fable*?
2. Do you know any fables or folktales from your native country? Which ones?

2 Read

SELF-STUDY
AUDIO CD **Read** the fable. Listen and read again.

~ All Things Are Connected ~

Long ago, there was a village chief who never allowed anyone to disagree with him. Whenever he wanted to do something, he asked the members of his court for their advice. But whether the chief's idea was wise or foolish, his advisors always said the same thing: "Indeed, it is wise." Only one old woman dared to give a different answer. Whenever the chief asked for her advice, she always replied, "All things are connected."

One night, the chief was awakened by the sound of frogs croaking in the swamp. It happened again the next night and the next and the next. The chief decided to kill all the frogs in the swamp. When he consulted the members of his court, they replied as usual: "Indeed, it is wise." But the old woman kept silent. "And you, old woman, what do you think?" the chief demanded. "All things are connected," she replied. The chief concluded that the old woman was a fool, and he ordered his servants to kill all the frogs. As a result, the chief slept peacefully.

But soon the mosquitoes in the swamp began to multiply since there were no frogs to eat them. They came into the village and made everyone miserable. The chief ordered his servants to go into the swamp and kill the mosquitoes, but it was impossible. Furious, the chief summoned the members of his court and blamed them, saying, "Why didn't you tell me that killing the frogs would make the mosquitoes multiply and everyone would be miserable? I should have listened to the old woman."

Due to the mosquitoes, all the people of the village were forced to go away. Finally, the chief and his family left, too. Until he died, the chief never forgot the old woman's words: "All things are connected."

3 After you read

A Check your understanding.

1. Why couldn't the chief sleep?
2. What did he decide to do?
3. What did the members of his court say?
4. What did the old woman say?
5. What did the servants do?
6. What happened as a result?
7. Why was the chief furious?
8. Why did the people leave the village?
9. After reading the story, what does the title mean to you?

Ask yourself questions when you read to identify a cause-and-effect relationship.

- To find an effect, ask, "What happened?"
- To find a cause, ask, "Why did it happen?"

B Build your vocabulary.

1. Underline the words from the chart in the reading passage.

2. Use a dictionary or a thesaurus. Write the part of speech. Write a synonym for each word. A synonym is a word that has the same or similar meaning.

3. Work in a small group. Write sentences with the synonyms.

Word	Part of speech	Synonym
wise	*adjective*	*sensible*
replied		
connected		
peacefully		
multiply		
miserable		
furious		

C Talk with a partner.

1. Do you think it is wise to follow other people's advice? Why or why not?
2. Give examples to show how plants and animals are connected.
3. How can people solve their conflicts peacefully?
4. What kind of weather makes you miserable?
5. What makes you furious?

Writing

1 Before you write

A Talk with a partner. Look at the picture. Answer the questions.

1. What is the environmental problem in this photo?
2. Why is it a problem? (causes)
3. How does this problem hurt people and the environment? (effects)

B Read the paragraph.

The Causes and Effects of Smog

Smog is a serious environmental problem in my city. One cause is that there are too many cars on the roads and highways. Most of the cars have only one person – the driver. People seem to take a lot of unnecessary trips. They drive to the drugstore instead of walking two blocks. Another cause of smog in my city is that we use too much electricity. Since many homes are not energy-efficient, our city's power plant has to produce more electricity. The burning coal from the power plant produces more air pollution. Due to the smog, the air is hard to breathe. Consequently, on many days it is unsafe for children and senior citizens to be outside. Smog also kills many trees and plants that produce oxygen and clean the air. If people drove less and used less electricity, I am sure our air quality would improve.

> One way to organize a paragraph is to discuss the causes and effects of a problem.

C Work with a partner. Complete the outline of the model paragraph.

Problem: Smog

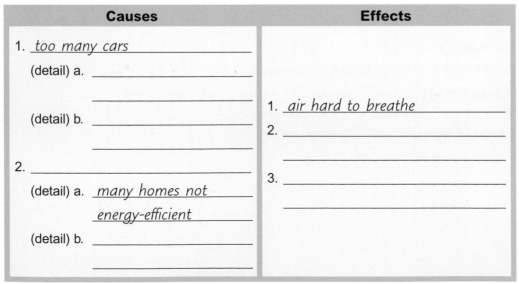

Causes	Effects
1. *too many cars*	
(detail) a. _____	
_____	1. *air hard to breathe*
(detail) b. _____	2. _____
_____	_____
2. _____	3. _____
(detail) a. *many homes not*	_____
energy-efficient	
(detail) b. _____	
_____	

D Plan a paragraph about an environmental problem in your city or community. Include the cause(s) and effect(s) of the problem. Use the outline to make notes on your ideas.

Problem: _____

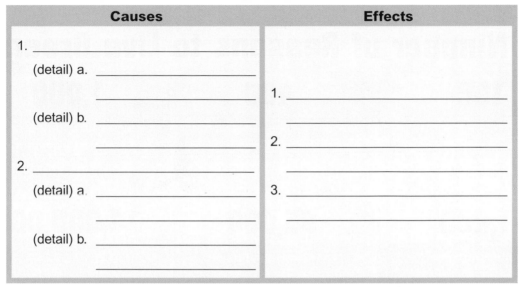

Causes	Effects
1. _____	
(detail) a. _____	
_____	1. _____
(detail) b. _____	
_____	2. _____
2. _____	
(detail) a. _____	3. _____
_____	
(detail) b. _____	
_____	

2 Write

Write a paragraph about an environmental problem in your city or community. Use the paragraph in Exercise 1B and the outlines in Exercises 1C and 1D to help you.

3 After you write

A Check your writing.

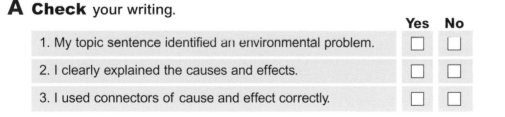

	Yes	No
1. My topic sentence identified an environmental problem.	☐	☐
2. I clearly explained the causes and effects.	☐	☐
3. I used connectors of cause and effect correctly.	☐	☐

B Share your writing with a partner.

1. Take turns. Read your paragraph to a partner.
2. Comment on your partner's paragraph. Ask your partner a question about the paragraph. Tell your partner one thing you learned.

Another view

1 Life-skills reading

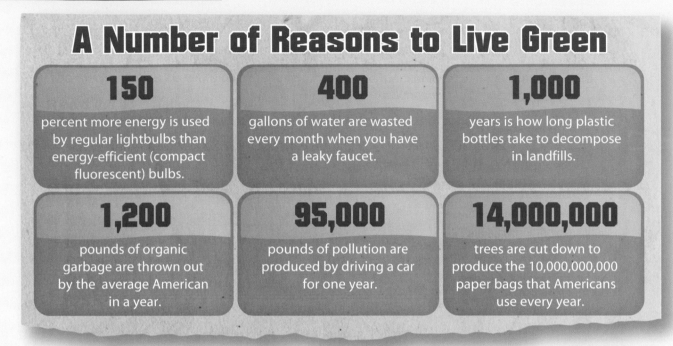

A Number of Reasons to Live Green

150	**400**	**1,000**
percent more energy is used by regular lightbulbs than energy-efficient (compact fluorescent) bulbs.	gallons of water are wasted every month when you have a leaky faucet.	years is how long plastic bottles take to decompose in landfills.

1,200	**95,000**	**14,000,000**
pounds of organic garbage are thrown out by the average American in a year.	pounds of pollution are produced by driving a car for one year.	trees are cut down to produce the 10,000,000,000 paper bags that Americans use every year.

A **Read** the questions. Look at the chart. Circle the answers.

1. How long do plastic bottles remain in landfills?
   a. 34 years
   b. 1,000 years
   c. 1,200 months
   d. none of the above

2. What does the number 95,000 represent?
   a. pounds of organic garbage thrown out
   b. pounds of smog from factories
   c. pounds of pollution from a car in one year
   d. none of the above

3. The number 400 represents _____ .
   a. dollars
   b. gallons
   c. months
   d. days

4. How much organic garbage is thrown out each year by the average American?
   a. 21 pounds
   b. 200 pounds
   c. 1,200 pounds
   d. 95,000 pounds

5. How many paper bags do Americans use every year?
   a. 10,000,000
   b. 14,000,000
   c. 10,000,000,000
   d. 14,000,000,000

6. What can you do to help the environment?
   a. Recycle plastic bottles.
   b. Fix faucets that leak.
   c. Replace regular lightbulbs with energy-efficient ones.
   d. all of the above

B **Talk** with your classmates. What do you do in your home to "live green"?

2 Fun with language

A **Talk** with a partner. Take the Living Green Quiz. Circle *true* or *false*. Then compare answers with your partner.

1. If you washed your dishes by hand instead of using a dishwasher, you would use less water.	true	false
2. The earth's temperature has risen almost 5 degrees Fahrenheit in the last 100 years.	true	false
3. Appliances that are plugged in use energy, even if they are turned off.	true	false
4. Alternative-fuel cars like hybrids are slower than conventional cars.	true	false
5. Energy-efficient lightbulbs last ten times longer than regular lightbulbs.	true	false
6. Driving in the city, you use 12 percent more gas if you drive with your air-conditioning on.	true	false
7. Most of global warming is due to natural causes; therefore, there is nothing people can do to prevent it.	true	false
8. If you turned down your heater by one degree, you would save about 5 percent per month on your heating bill.	true	false

Share answers with your classmates. Check with your teacher for the correct answers.

B **Work** with a partner. How many new words can you make with the letters from the word *environment*?

e-n-v-i-r-o-n-m-e-n-t

3 Wrap up

Complete the **Self-assessment** on page 145.

Lesson A *Get ready*

1 Talk about the pictures

A What do you see?

B What is happening?

2 Listening

SELF-STUDY AUDIO CD

A 🔊 **Listen** and answer the questions.

1. Who are the speakers?
2. What are they talking about?

SELF-STUDY AUDIO CD

B 🔊 **Listen again.** Complete the chart.

	American wedding customs	Vietnamese wedding customs
1. Gifts	*register in a store*	
2. Use of rice		*red sticky rice*
3. Dress color		

Listen again. Check your answers.

SELF-STUDY AUDIO CD

C 🔊 **Read.** Complete the story. Listen and check your answers.

acquaintances	fortune	reception	symbolizes
courses	looking forward	registered	tradition

Cathy and Thanh are talking about wedding customs. Cathy is invited to a Vietnamese wedding, and she is surprised that the bride and groom are not ___registered___ for gifts at any stores. In contrast, Thanh is surprised by the
₁

American _____ of throwing rice at the bride and groom. Next, they
₂

talk about clothes. Thanh says a Vietnamese bride wears a red dress because the

color red _____ good _____ . Then Cathy asks why she
₃   ₄

was invited only to the wedding _____ , not the ceremony. Thanh
₅

explains that traditionally the ceremony is only for the family. The couple's

friends and _____ are invited to the evening reception. In fact, Thanh
₆

says the evening party will include seven or eight _____ of food.
₇

Cathy says she is _____ to the wedding.
₈

D **Discuss.** Talk with your classmates.

1. Share some special wedding customs from your culture.
2. Have you ever attended an American wedding? What did you think about it?

Conditional sentences

1 Grammar focus: future real conditional and unreal conditional

Future real conditional (possible)

If I go to the wedding, I will wear my new shoes.

If Jane doesn't have to work that day, she will go to the wedding.

For a grammar explanation, turn to page 152.

Unreal conditional (not possible)

If I went to the wedding, I would wear my new shoes. (But I'm not going.)

If Jane didn't work that day, she would go to the wedding. (But Jane has to work.)

Useful language

The unreal conditional form of the verb *be* is **were**.

*If I **were** you, I would give them cash for their wedding.*

*If it **were** warmer, we could have the wedding outdoors.*

2 Practice

A Write. Complete the sentences. Use the future real or unreal conditional forms of the verbs.

1. The Patels are from India, but they live in the United States now. They are planning a wedding for their daughter, Parveen. If they ____lived____ in India, (live) the groom's family __would pay__ for the wedding. (pay)

2. The wedding will be in the United States. If the Patels _____ the wedding in India, the (have) wedding celebration _____ three days. Here (last) it will last for one day.

3. The Patels don't have a lot of money. If they _____ rich, they _____ 300 people; instead, they will invite about 150. (be) (invite)

4. The Patels are planning to have music for the reception. If a band _____ (not / charge) too much, they _____ live music. (have)

5. It's possible that the weather will be nice on the day of the wedding. If the weather _____ nice, they _____ the ceremony outside. (be) (have)

6. Parveen and her new husband will live in their own apartment. If they _____ (be) in India, they _____ with the groom's parents. (live)

Listen and check your answers.

B Talk with a partner. Take turns making sentences about Victor's real and imaginary plans for New Year's Eve.

> **A** If Victor stays home on New Year's Eve, he will have a party with his friends.
> **B** But if he traveled to Florida, he would spend New Year's Eve near the beach.

Real	Imaginary
stay home / have a party with his friends	travel to Florida / spend New Year's Eve near the beach
go to his parents' house / have a quiet celebration with family	be in Mexico / eat 12 grapes at midnight
travel to New York / celebrate New Year's Eve in Times Square	travel to Brazil / watch fireworks on the beach at midnight
go to a club / dance all night	be in France / have a special dinner

Write sentences about Victor's real and imaginary plans.

If Victor stays home on New Year's Eve, he will have a party with his friends.

If he traveled to Florida, he would spend New Year's Eve near the beach.

3 Communicate

A Talk with a partner. Complete the chart with your real and imaginary plans for some future holidays or special events.

Holiday or event	Real	Imaginary
New Year's Eve	*stay home*	*be in my native country*
birthday		
(your idea)		
(your idea)		

B Work in a small group. Share your charts. Ask and answer questions about each other's plans.

> **A** If you stay home on New Year's Eve, how will you celebrate?
> **B** If I stay home, I'll invite my friends to come over and celebrate with me.

> **A** If you were in your native country on New Year's Eve, how would you celebrate?
> **B** If I were in my native country, I would watch fireworks at midnight.

C Share information about your classmates.

Lesson C *Expressing hopes and wishes*

1 Grammar focus: *hope* and *wish*

Possible situations

Samira hopes her cousin will come to her wedding.
Samira hopes her cousin comes to her wedding.
Nick hopes he can go to the party.

Situations that are not possible

Samira wishes her cousin would come to her wedding.
Nick wishes he could go to the party.

For a grammar explanation, turn to page 153.

Useful language

In expressing hopes, using the modal *will* or the simple present tense are both correct.
I hope you will attend.
I hope you attend.

2 Practice

A Write. Complete the sentences. Use *hopes* or *wishes* and the correct form of the verb or modal.

1. Paul's high school graduation is tomorrow.

   His friend Luis has to work. Luis ___wishes___ he

   ___could go___ to Paul's graduation.
   (can go)

2. Paul's father has asked for the day off so that

   he can attend his son's graduation. He _____

   he _____ the day off.
   (get)

3. Paul's grandfather has been sick. He's not sure if he will attend the graduation.

   Paul _____ his grandfather _____ the ceremony.
   (will attend)

4. The graduation ceremony will be outside. Paul _____ it _____ .
   (will not / rain)

5. Paul's mother would like to buy him a new car, but she can't afford it.

   She _____ she _____ him a new car.
   (can buy)

6. Paul wasn't accepted to the university, so he will go to a community college.

   Paul _____ he _____ to the university.
   (can go)

7. It's possible that Paul will be able to transfer to the university in two years.

   He _____ he _____ in two years.
   (can transfer)

   Listen and check your answers.

B Talk with a partner. Read the situations. Make statements with *hope* or *wish*.

> Ryan wants to get a new cell phone as a birthday gift.

> Ryan hopes he will get a new cell phone as a birthday gift.

1. Ryan wants to get a new cell phone as a birthday gift.
2. Soraya can't go home for Thanksgiving because she has to work.
3. Marla wants to have a big graduation party, but her apartment is too small.
4. Avi is trying to get a plane reservation so that he can attend his cousin's wedding in Las Vegas.
5. Karl plans to ask Marta to marry him next weekend. He doesn't know if she will say yes.
6. Maria wants to marry Jeffrey, but she knows that he doesn't love her.
7. Anton and Ilsa are expecting a baby. They want the baby to be healthy.

Write a sentence for each situation.

Ryan hopes he will get a new cell phone as a birthday gift.

3 Communicate

A Write three holidays or celebrations that you observe. Think about something you wish you could change about each one.

Mother's Day: *I wish I could have the day off to be with my children.*

1. _____: _____

_____

2. _____: _____

_____

3. _____: _____

_____

B Work in a small group. Talk about your wishes. Listen to your classmates' hopes for you.

> *A* I don't have Mother's Day off. I wish I could have the day off to be with my children.
> *B* I hope you get the day off next year.
> *C* I hope your children will do something special for you.

Useful language

Expressing hope is a common way of ending a conversation.

I hope you feel better soon.

I hope you have a good time.

C Share information about your classmates.

1 Before you read

Talk with your classmates. Answer the questions.

1. How are birthdays usually celebrated in your culture?
2. Are some birthdays more special than others? Which ones?

2 Read

SELF-STUDY
AUDIO CD

Read the magazine article. Listen and read again.

Special Birthdays Around the World

In most cultures, there are certain birthdays that are especially important in a young person's life. If you were an American teenager, for example, you would eagerly look forward to your 16th birthday because in most states that is the age to get a driver's license. Other cultures also have birthdays with special meanings:

A girl's quinceañera

Mexico For Mexican girls, the 15th birthday – the "Quinceañera" – symbolizes a girl's transition into adulthood. To celebrate, the girl's family throws a huge party. The girl wears a ball gown similar to a wedding dress. The girl performs a waltz, a formal dance, with her father.

China On a child's first birthday, parents place their baby in the center of a group of objects, such as a shiny coin, a book, and a doll. Then they watch to see which object the baby picks up first. Most parents hope their child will pick up the coin because, according to tradition, it means the child will be rich.

Nigeria The 1st, 5th, 10th, and 15th birthdays are considered extremely important. Parties are held with up to 100 people. The guests enjoy a feast of a roasted cow or goat.

Japan A girl's 3rd and 7th birthdays and a boy's 5th birthday are considered special. In a ceremony known as "7, 5, 3," children wear their best kimonos (ceremonial gowns) and receive bags of sweets with "sweets for 1,000 years of life" written on them.

Israel A boy's 13th and a girl's 12th birthdays are serious as well as happy occasions. On these birthdays, children become responsible for their own religious and moral behavior.

Adult birthdays also have special significance in many cultures. In the United States, for example, birthdays ending in "0" – 30, 40, 50, etc. – are especially meaningful.

3 After you read

A Check your understanding.

1. Why do American teenagers look forward to their 16th birthdays?
2. What is the Spanish name for a girl's 15th birthday?
3. What is a waltz?
4. What is a kimono?
5. Which birthdays are especially meaningful in the United States?
6. Are any of the special birthdays described in the reading similar to traditions in your culture?

> Punctuation can be a clue to meaning. For example, parentheses, commas, and dashes are all used to mark definitions, examples, or explanations.

B Build your vocabulary.

1. Underline the words from the chart in the reading passage. Write the meaning from the story.

2. Use a dictionary and write a different meaning of each word.

3. Write sentences using the other meaning of each word.

Word in story	Meaning in story	Other meaning
1. states	areas that are part of a country	conditions of the mind
2. object		
3. rich		
4. transition		
5. throw		
6. party		
7. ball		

C Talk with a partner.

1. How many states are there in your native country?
2. Do you have a favorite object? What is it? Why do you like it?
3. What transitions have you made in your life?
4. Have you ever thrown a large party? What was the occasion?
5. Have you ever attended a ball? If so, what did you wear?

1 Before you write

A Talk with a partner.

1. Look at the pictures. Can you guess where the people are from and what holiday they are celebrating?

2. What is your favorite holiday or celebration? Why?

B Read the paragraph.

My Favorite Celebration

My favorite celebration is the Iranian New Year, *Norouz* ("new day"). This holiday begins on the first day of spring and lasts 13 days. On the Wednesday before Norouz, people build bonfires and jump over them. Iranian people believe that if they do this, they will get rid of their illnesses and misfortunes. On Norouz Eve, the family gathers around a table with seven items that begin with the letter "s" in Persian: an apple, wheat pudding, dried berries, vinegar, a coin, a beautiful flower, and garlic. A bowl of goldfish, a Koran, colored eggs, and a mirror are also on the table. These items symbolize beauty, health, prosperity, and fertility. On Norouz Day, people kiss each other and say, "I hope you will live for one hundred years." We spend the next 13 days visiting each other and eating sweets. Finally, on the last day of the celebration, everyone goes to a park for a big picnic. I wish my whole family lived with me here so that we could celebrate Norouz together.

The conclusion is an important part of a paragraph. One way to conclude a paragraph is to relate the topic to your personal life.

C Work with a partner. Complete the outline of the model paragraph.

    I. Topic: *My Favorite Celebration – Norouz* _____

    II. Meaning or symbolism: _____

    _____

    III. When celebrated: _____

    IV. Customs:

        A. _____

        B. _____

        C. _____

        D. _____

        E. _____

    V. Conclusion: _____

    _____

D Plan a paragraph about your favorite holiday or celebration. Make an outline like the one in Exercise 1C. Include at least three customs. Use your own paper.

2 Write

Write a paragraph about your favorite holiday or celebration. Use the paragraph in Exercise 1B and the outlines in Exercises 1C and 1D to help you.

3 After you write

A Check your writing.

	Yes	No
1. I described at least three customs for my favorite holiday or celebration.	☐	☐
2. I wrote a conclusion relating the celebration to my personal life.	☐	☐
3. I used *hope* and *wish* correctly.	☐	☐

B Share your writing with a partner.

1. Take turns. Read your paragraph to a partner.
2. Comment on your partner's paragraph. Ask your partner a question about the paragraph. Tell your partner one thing you learned.

1 Life-skills reading

Pumpkin Pie

Preparation time: 15 minutes
Cooking time: 50 minutes

Ingredients

1 pre-made pie crust
1 (8-ounce) package cream
  cheese, softened
2 cups canned pumpkin,
  mashed

¼ teaspoon salt
1 cup sugar
1 egg plus 2 egg yolks,
  lightly beaten
1 cup heavy cream

¼ cup (½ stick) melted butter
1 teaspoon vanilla extract
½ teaspoon ground cinnamon
¼ teaspoon ground ginger,
  optional

1. Preheat the oven to 350 degrees Fahrenheit.
2. Beat the softened cream cheese.
3. Add the pumpkin and beat until blended.
4. Then add the salt and sugar, and beat until blended.
5. Then add the egg mixed with the yolks, cream, and melted butter, and beat until blended.
6. Finally, mix in the vanilla, cinnamon, and ginger.

7. Pour the filling into the pre-made pie crust, and bake for 50 minutes, or until the center is firm.
8. Set the pie on a wire rack, and cool until it is room temperature. Cut into slices and serve with whipped cream or ice cream.

Serves 6–8 people.

A Read the questions. Look at the recipe. Circle the answers.

1. How much sugar do you need to make the pie?
   a. ¼ cup
   b. ½ cup
   c. 1 cup
   d. 2 cups

2. What is the total cooking time for the pie?
   a. 10 minutes
   b. 15 minutes
   c. 30 minutes
   d. 50 minutes

3. Which of the following statements is true?
   a. Soften the butter.
   b. Use 1 cup of milk.
   c. Use 1 stick of butter.
   d. Beat the eggs.

4. What should you do after you blend the cream cheese and pumpkin?
   a. Add the salt and sugar.
   b. Bake the pie.
   c. Add the eggs.
   d. Pour the filling into the pie crust.

5. How many people does this recipe serve?
   a. 1–2
   b. 3–4
   c. 5–6
   d. 6–8

6. Which ingredient is not required?
   a. vanilla
   b. ginger
   c. cinnamon
   d. cream cheese

B Talk with a partner. What is a traditional meal or recipe for a celebration in your native country? Describe the meal or recipe to your partner.

2 Fun with language

Green Day: Keep Our Cities Green

A Day of NO Driving

GREEN

Lemonade+Cupcakes

A Work in a small group. Design a new holiday or celebration. Use the outline as a guide to organize your group's ideas.

I. Origin
   A. What is the name of the holiday or celebration?
   B. When is it? What month and day(s)? How long does it last?
   C. Describe the holiday or celebration. Is there some history behind it? Why is it celebrated? What does it symbolize?
   D. Who celebrates the holiday – everyone? only children?

II. Location
   A. Where is it celebrated – outside? inside?
   B. Are there special places to visit or go to?

III. Traditions
   A. What are three customs related to the holiday?
   B. Are any special clothes worn or foods eaten?

Share your holiday or celebration with your classmates.

B Work with a partner. Share greetings for important holidays.

In the United States, people say "Happy New Year" on January 1.

1. Holiday: _____   Greeting: _____
2. Holiday: _____   Greeting: _____

Share information with your classmates.

3 Wrap up

Complete the **Self-assessment** on page 145.

Review

1 Listening

🔵 **Listen.** Take notes on a street interview.

Things that bring good luck	Things that bring bad luck
1. *wear bright colors like red*	4.
2.	5.
3.	6.

Talk with a partner. Check your answers.

2 Grammar

A Write. Complete the story.

A New Year's Eve Celebration

Sergei _____*wishes*_____ his friend Olga could visit him in New York

1. hopes / wishes

over the holidays, but she can't get the time off. _____ , they

2. Consequently / Since

won't be together on New Year's Eve. If she _____ in New York,

3. is / were

he would take her to Times Square _____ the big celebration

4. since / because of

there. Every year at one minute before midnight, a large crystal ball starts to

drop slowly from high above the street. When it reaches the bottom, everybody

goes crazy _____ it's the beginning of the New Year. Sergei

5. since / due to

really _____ that Olga can come next year. If she comes, she

6. hopes / wishes

_____ have a great time.

7. will / would

B Write. Look at the words that are underlined in the answers. Write
the questions.

1. **A** _____

   B Sergei would take Olga to <u>Times Square</u> if she were in New York.

2. **A** _____

   B <u>The crystal ball</u> starts to drop at one minute before midnight.

3. **A** _____

   B Sergei hopes that Olga can come <u>next year</u>.

Talk with a partner. Ask and answer the questions.

3 Pronunciation: identifying thought groups

Thought groups are phrases that usually have one strongly stressed word. A sentence can have several thought groups that are separated by short pauses.

A 💿 **Listen** to the following sentences.

One thought group
1. We need to save <u>energy</u>.
2. I always take the <u>bus</u> to work.

Two thought groups
3. We need to <u>reduce</u> our energy use / and <u>protect</u> the environment.
4. When I lived in <u>Vietnam</u>, / I always <u>walked</u> to work.

Three or more thought groups
5. There are <u>several</u> things you can do / to <u>reduce</u> your energy use / and <u>protect</u> the environment.
6. You can <u>walk</u>, / ride a <u>bicycle</u>, / <u>carpool</u>, / or take the <u>bus</u>.

💿 **Listen again and repeat.** Pay attention to the thought groups and pauses.

B 💿 **Listen and repeat.** Then put slash marks (/) between the thought groups.

1. People are very concerned about the environment.
2. We need to take responsibility for saving the earth.
3. There are many ways that we can save energy.
4. One thing people can do is to cut down on their driving.
5. And also, we need to be careful not to waste electricity.
6. We can get a lot of information about global warming on the Internet.

Talk with a partner. Compare your answers.

C **Talk** with a partner. Practice the questions and answers. Divide each sentence into thought groups.

1. *A* Have you read about global warming?
   B Yes, I've read a lot about it.

2. *A* What uses more energy, your stove or your refrigerator?
   B I'm not sure, but I think my refrigerator uses more energy because it's 15 years old.

3. *A* What do guests bring to a Vietnamese wedding?
   B At a Vietnamese wedding, the guests just bring cash.

4. *A* What do people do on the last day of the celebration?
   B On the last day, everyone goes to a park for a big picnic.

D **Write** four questions about saving energy. Ask your partner.

Projects

A job for your intelligence

A Use the Internet.

Find careers that match your primary intelligence.

Keywords (your primary intelligence), intelligence, careers

B Make a chart.

Make a list of careers that match your primary intelligence. Are you interested in any of them? Check your opinion.

Careers for bodily / kinesthetic intelligence	Interested	Not interested
carpenter		✓
actor	✓	
dancer		✓
landscaper	✓	

C Share your information.

Talk about your chart. Explain why you are or are not interested in the careers that match your primary intelligence.
Listen as your classmates present their charts. Suggest other careers for them.

Continuing education

A Find information about a class.

Look at a course catalog or class schedule from an adult school or community college. Find two classes you would like to take. Copy or print out the course description.

B Take notes. Answer these questions.

1. What are the class names?
2. When are the classes scheduled?
3. Where are they located?
4. What are the requirements, if any?
5. How much do the classes cost?

Class	Dates	Time	Location	Requirements	Cost
Culinary Arts 1	Jan. 15–Mar. 2	M–F: 8:30–2:30	ECC, Room 129	placement test	$95

C Share your information.

Tell your classmates about the classes you chose. Why did you choose them? Are you going to take them? Why or why not?

Household rules

A Make a list.

Write some rules that children should follow at home.

> Do homework.
> Take off shoes in the house.
> Help with chores around the house.

B Interview a partner.

Find more rules that children should follow. Add them to your list.

C Share your information.

Make a class wall chart.
Talk about the rules. Which ones are for young children (5 to 12 years old)?
Which ones are for teenagers? Are some rules too strict? Which ones?

Coping with test anxiety

A Use the Internet.

Find information about ways to cope with anxiety before or during tests.

Keywords | anxiety before tests | | test anxiety |

B Make a list.

Write ways to cope with anxiety
before or during tests.

1. Get a good night's sleep before the test.

2. Come to class early on the day of the test, so you have time to relax.

3. Get comfortable in your chair.

C Share your information.

Talk to your classmates about ways to cope
with test anxiety.
Make a class poster.
What are the best ideas? Take a class vote.

Helping others

A Think about helping.

What are some things that people have done to help you? Share your experiences with a partner.

B Make a list.

Write the names of the people you have helped. What did you do to help them?

Person	What did you do to help?
My grandmother	took her to her doctor's appointment
My neighbor	cut his grass
My friend Donna	helped her with her homework

C Share your information.

Talk to your classmates about helping others.
Make a class wall chart of ways to help.

Time-saving devices

A Use the Internet.

Find information about a time-saving device you have or would like to have.

Keywords (name of time-saving device) time-saving devices

B Take notes. Answer these questions.

1. Who invented it?
2. When was it invented?
3. What are some interesting things about this device?

Device	Who invented it?	When was it invented?	Interesting things
washing machine	Hamilton Smith	1858	There is a Washing Machine Museum in Colorado.

C Share your information.

Talk about the device.
Make a class wall chart.
Take a class survey. Which time-saving device do most of your classmates have?
Which one would most of them like to have?

What's the return policy?

A Find three ads or store receipts that show a store's return policy.

Underline the important information.

B Make a chart.

Write the name of the store and the return policy for that store.

Store	Return policy
Alta's Dress Shop	Receipt required for refund.
Jack's Secondhand Bookstore	Store credit or exchanges only.
Dickenson's Electronics	No returns after 30 days.

C Share your information.

Show your chart to your classmates.
Which store has the best return policy?
Which store has the worst return policy?

Tips for cover letters

A Use the Internet.

Find information about how to write a good cover letter.

Keywords | how to write a cover letter | | cover letter writing tips |

B Take notes.

1. Write three tips.
2. Print out a sample cover letter.

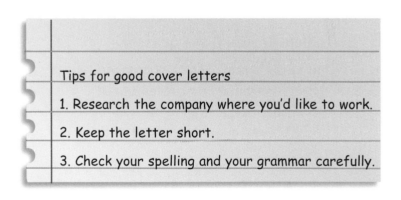

Tips for good cover letters

1. Research the company where you'd like to work.

2. Keep the letter short.

3. Check your spelling and your grammar carefully.

C Share your information.

Show the cover letter to your classmates.
Tell them why you think it's a good cover letter.
Make a class book of good cover letters.

"Green" tips for school

A Make a list.

What are some ways your school could be "green"? Write your ideas.

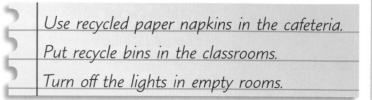

Use recycled paper napkins in the cafeteria.

Put recycle bins in the classrooms.

Turn off the lights in empty rooms.

B Interview a partner.

Find two more ideas for "living green" at school. Add them to your list.

C Share your information.

Make a class poster.
Invite a school administrator to your classroom.
Share your class poster with the administrator.

Celebrations around the world

A Use the Internet.

Choose a holiday or celebration. Find information about the way it is celebrated in another country.

Keywords (holiday or celebration), customs around the world

B Take notes. Answer these questions.

1. What is the name of the celebration?
2. What is the country you researched?
3. What is the background or reason for the celebration?
4. What are some customs related to this holiday or celebration?

Celebration	Country	Background	Customs
Independence Day	Peru	Peru declared its independence from Spain on July 28, 1821.	People have two days off. The president gives a speech. There are parades. Families spend time together.

C Share your information.

Tell your class about the holiday or celebration you researched.
Make a class book.

Self-assessments

Unit 1 Personal information

A Vocabulary Write eight new words you have learned.

_____ _____ _____ _____

_____ _____ _____ _____

B Skills and functions Read the sentences. Rate yourself. Circle 3 (*I agree.*) OR
2 (*I'm not sure.*) OR 1 (*I can't do this.*).

I can use noun clauses to talk about what I think: *I believe that every person is unique.*	3	2	1
I can use adjectives and adverbs: *She's a good writer. She writes well.*	3	2	1
I can skim an article to get a general idea of what it is about.	3	2	1
I can write a paragraph with a general topic sentence and supporting details.	3	2	1
I can read and understand a diagram.	3	2	1

C What's next? Choose one.

☐ I am ready for the unit test.   ☐ I need more practice with _____ .

Unit 2 At school

A Vocabulary Write eight new words you have learned.

_____ _____ _____ _____

_____ _____ _____ _____

B Skills and functions Read the sentences. Rate yourself. Circle 3 (*I agree.*) OR
2 (*I'm not sure.*) OR 1 (*I can't do this.*).

I can ask and answer questions with the present passive: *Are internships offered for this program? Yes, internships are offered.*	3	2	1
I can use the present passive with infinitives: *The student is required to take a placement test.*	3	2	1
I can scan an article to find specific information.	3	2	1
I can write a paragraph using specific details such as facts, examples, and reasons to support my topic sentence.	3	2	1
I can read and understand a chart.	3	2	1

C What's next? Choose one.

☐ I am ready for the unit test.   ☐ I need more practice with _____ .

Unit 3 Friends and family

A Vocabulary Write eight new words you have learned.

_____   _____   _____   _____

_____   _____   _____   _____

B Skills and functions Read the sentences. Rate yourself. Circle 3 (*I agree.*) OR
2 (*I'm not sure.*) OR 1 (*I can't do this.*).

I can ask indirect *Wh-* questions: *I'd like to know **why Maria is** so strict. Can you tell me **why Maria is** so strict?*	3 2 1
I can ask indirect *Yes / No* questions: *I'd like to know **if you finished** your homework. Can you tell me **whether you finished** your homework?*	3 2 1
I can recognize words that are repeated to get an idea of what a reading is about.	3 2 1
I can write a paragraph using transition words to show the relationship between sentences or ideas in a paragraph.	3 2 1
I can read and understand a survey.	3 2 1

C What's next? Choose one.

☐ I am ready for the unit test.   ☐ I need more practice with _____ .

Unit 4 Health

A Vocabulary Write eight new words you have learned.

_____   _____   _____   _____

_____   _____   _____   _____

B Skills and functions Read the sentences. Rate yourself. Circle 3 (*I agree.*) OR
2 (*I'm not sure.*) OR 1 (*I can't do this.*).

I can make sentences with *ought to, shouldn't, have to,* and *don't have to* to express advice, necessity, or lack of necessity.	3 2 1
I can use *should have* and *shouldn't have* to talk about regrets and advice in the past.	3 2 1
I can relate what I read to my own experience.	3 2 1
I can write a paragraph organized by actions and results.	3 2 1
I can read and understand a bar graph.	3 2 1

C What's next? Choose one.

☐ I am ready for the unit test.   ☐ I need more practice with _____ .

Unit 5 Around town

A Vocabulary Write eight new words you have learned.

_____   _____   _____   _____

_____   _____   _____   _____

B Skills and functions Read the sentences. Rate yourself. Circle 3 (*I agree.*) OR
2 (*I'm not sure.*) OR 1 (*I can't do this.*).

I can make sentences with the time clauses *until* and *as soon as*: She stayed **until** he finished lunch. She left **as soon as** he finished lunch.	3 2 1
I can make sentences with repeated actions in the present and past: *She* **volunteers** *three times a month.* She **has volunteered** *several times this month.*	3 2 1
I can guess if a word is positive or negative by reading the words around it.	3 2 1
I can write a paragraph with details answering *Wh-* questions.	3 2 1
I can read and understand advertisements for volunteer positions.	3 2 1

C What's next? Choose one.

☐ I am ready for the unit test.   ☐ I need more practice with _____ .

Unit 6 Time

A Vocabulary Write eight new words you have learned.

_____   _____   _____   _____

_____   _____   _____   _____

B Skills and functions Read the sentences. Rate yourself. Circle 3 (*I agree.*) OR
2 (*I'm not sure.*) OR 1 (*I can't do this.*).

I can make sentences with *although* and *even though*: I drive **although** the subway is cheaper. I drive **even though** the subway is cheaper.	3 2 1
I can distinguish between *because* and *although*: I drive **because** it is convenient. I drive **although** gas is expensive.	3 2 1
I can distinguish between fact and opinion.	3 2 1
I can write a paragraph describing advantages and disadvantages.	3 2 1
I can read and understand a table.	3 2 1

C What's next? Choose one.

☐ I am ready for the unit test.   ☐ I need more practice with _____ .

Unit 7 Shopping

A Vocabulary Write eight new words you have learned.

_____   _____   _____   _____

_____   _____   _____   _____

B Skills and functions Read the sentences. Rate yourself. Circle 3 (*I agree.*) OR
2 (*I'm not sure.*) OR 1 (*I can't do this.*).

I can use adjective clauses as the subject of a dependent clause: *I want to get a camera **that's not too expensive**.*	3	2	1
I can use adjective clauses as the object of a dependent clause: *I like the car **that you bought**.*	3	2	1
I can recognize synonyms in a reading.	3	2	1
I can write a paragraph using transition words to signal a list of reasons.	3	2	1
I can read and understand a returned-merchandise form.	3	2	1

C What's next? Choose one.

☐ I am ready for the unit test.   ☐ I need more practice with _____ .

Unit 8 Work

A Vocabulary Write eight new words you have learned.

_____   _____   _____   _____

_____   _____   _____   _____

B Skills and functions Read the sentences. Rate yourself. Circle 3 (*I agree.*) OR
2 (*I'm not sure.*) OR 1 (*I can't do this.*).

I can use the present perfect and the present perfect continuous: *He **has just talked** to the manager.* *He **has been talking** to the manager for several minutes.*	3	2	1
I can use adjectives ending in *-ed* and *-ing* to describe feelings or characteristics: *She's **excited**. The job is **exciting**.*	3	2	1
I can recognize how quotations are used to support the main idea.	3	2	1
I can write a cover letter that includes all the important information.	3	2	1
I can read and understand a chart.	3	2	1

C What's next? Choose one.

☐ I am ready for the unit test.   ☐ I need more practice with _____ .

Unit 9 Daily living

A Vocabulary Write eight new words you have learned.

_____   _____   _____   _____

_____   _____   _____   _____

B Skills and functions Read the sentences. Rate yourself. Circle 3 (*I agree.*) OR
2 (*I'm not sure.*) OR 1 (*I can't do this.*).

I can make sentences using the present unreal conditional: *If everybody **drove** smaller cars, we **would use** less gasoline.*	3 2 1
I can use *since, due to, consequently,* and *as a result* to show cause and effect: ***Since** the earth is getting warmer, the polar ice caps are melting.* *The earth is getting warmer. **Consequently**, the polar ice caps are melting.*	3 2 1
I can ask myself questions when I read to identify a cause-and-effect relationship.	3 2 1
I can write a paragraph describing the causes and effects of a problem.	3 2 1
I can read and understand a chart.	3 2 1

C What's next? Choose one.

☐ I am ready for the unit test.   ☐ I need more practice with _____ .

Unit 10 Leisure

A Vocabulary Write eight new words you have learned.

_____   _____   _____   _____

_____   _____   _____   _____

B Skills and functions Read the sentences. Rate yourself. Circle 3 (*I agree.*) OR
2 (*I'm not sure.*) OR 1 (*I can't do this.*).

I can make statements using the future real conditional and unreal conditional: *If I **have** time, I **will call** you. If I **had** time, I **would call** you.*	3 2 1
I can make statements using *hope* and *wish*: *I **hope** I **can come** to the party. I **wish** I **could come** to the party.*	3 2 1
I can recognize punctuation in a reading that gives a clue to meaning.	3 2 1
I can write a conclusion that relates the topic to my personal life.	3 2 1
I can read and understand a recipe.	3 2 1

C What's next? Choose one.

☐ I am ready for the unit test.   ☐ I need more practice with _____ .

Reference

Clauses

A *clause* is a part of a sentence that has a subject and a verb.
A *main clause* is a complete sentence.
A *dependent clause* is not a complete sentence; it is connected to a main clause.
A sentence with the structure main clause + dependent clause or
dependent clause + main clause is called a *complex sentence*.

Noun clauses with *that*

Some complex sentences have the form main clause + noun clause (see Clauses above).
A noun clause is a type of dependent clause. Some noun clauses consist of *that* + subject + verb.
However, it is also correct to omit *that*. The main clause can be a statement or a question.

	Main clause	Noun clause
Statement	People think	(that) she is smart.
Question	Do you think	(that) she is smart?

Adjectives and adverbs

Adjectives give information about nouns.
Adverbs give information about verbs. Most adverbs end in *-ly*.
A few adverbs are irregular, such as *fast*, *well*, and *hard*.

Adjective	Regular adverb	Irregular adverb
Carol is an *intelligent* girl.	Carol speaks *intelligently*.	Carol speaks *well*.

Sometimes the same word can be an adjective or an adverb.

Adjective	Adverb
It's a *hard* test. John is a *fast* worker.	John works *hard* and *fast*.

Present passive

Active sentences have the form subject + verb + object. Passive sentences have the form subject + *be* + past participle. The object of an active sentence becomes the subject of a passive sentence. An active verb is used to say what the subject does. A passive verb is used to say what happens to the subject. A phrase consisting of *by* + noun comes after the passive verb if it is important to know who performs an action. More often, the passive is used without the *by* phrase.

See page 154 for a list of irregular past participles.

Affirmative statements

Active		Passive
The college gives an English placement test twice a year.	Singular	An English placement test is given (by the college) twice a year.
The college offers online classes every semester.	Plural	Online classes are offered every semester.

Yes / No questions

Active		Passive
Does the college offer financial aid?	Singular	Is financial aid offered (by the college)?
Does the college give online courses every semester?	Plural	Are online courses given every semester (by the college)?

Wh- questions

Active		Passive
When does the college give the placement test?	Singular	When is the placement test given (by the college)?
Where does the college hold English classes?	Plural	Where are English classes held (by the college)?

Infinitives after passive verbs

Some passive verbs can have an infinitive after them.

Active	Passive
The teacher tells the students to bring a dictionary to class.	The students are told (by the teacher) to bring a dictionary to class.

Verbs often followed by infinitives

advise	intend	require
allow	mean	tell
encourage	plan	use
expect	prepare	

Direct and indirect questions

A *direct* question is a complete sentence. An *indirect* question is a dependent clause (see Clauses on page 146). It comes after a main clause. The main clause can be a statement or a question. If it is a question, a question mark is used at the end of the sentence. Indirect *wh-* questions begin with question words (*who, what, where, when, why, how*). Indirect *yes / no* questions begin with *if* or *whether*. *Whether* is more formal.

Wh- questions

	Direct	Indirect
Present	When does the bus come?	Do you know when the bus comes?
Past	Where did she go?	Please tell me where she went.

Yes / No questions

	Direct	Indirect
Present	Do they have a test today?	Do you know if they have a test today? Do you know whether they have a test today?
Past	Did he finish his homework?	I wonder if he finished his homework. I'd like to know whether he finished his homework.

Common introductory clauses that are used with indirect questions

I'd like to know . . .	I wonder . . .	Do you have any idea . . . ?
I don't know . . .	Please explain . . .	Can you tell me . . . ?
I want to know . . .	Tell me . . .	Do you know . . . ?
I need to know . . .		

Present modals: *ought to, shouldn't, have to, don't have to*

Ought to is the same as *should*. It is used to give advice. *Shouldn't* is the opposite of both *ought to* and *should*. *Have to / Has to* mean that it is necessary to do something. The subject has no choice about it. *Don't have to / Doesn't have to* mean that it is not necessary to do something. The subject can choose to do it or not.

Affirmative statements

I You We They	ought to have to	relax.
He She	ought to has to	relax.

Negative statements

I You We They	shouldn't don't have to	work so hard.
He She	shouldn't doesn't have to	work so hard.

Past modals: *should have, shouldn't have*

Should have / *Shouldn't have* + past participle mean that the speaker is sorry about (regrets) something he or she did or did not do in the past. These modals can also be used to give advice about something in the past.

<table>
<tr><td colspan="3">Affirmative statements</td><td colspan="3">Negative statements</td></tr>
<tr>
<td>I
You
He
She
We
You
They</td>
<td>should have</td>
<td>left earlier.</td>
<td>I
You
He
She
We
You
They</td>
<td>shouldn't have</td>
<td>eaten so much.</td>
</tr>
</table>

Time clauses with *until* and *as soon as*

Dependent time clauses with *until* and *as soon as* can come at the beginning or end of a sentence. Use a comma (,) after a time clause that comes at the beginning of a sentence.

until	Use *until* in the dependent clause to say how long an action continues. *Until* the patient finished his lunch, the nurse stayed with him. The nurse stayed with the patient *until* he finished his lunch.
as soon as	Use *as soon as* in the dependent clause to mean "right after." *As soon as* the patient finished his lunch, the nurse left. The nurse left *as soon as* the patient finished his lunch.

Time words and expressions to describe repeated actions

In sentences that talk about repeated actions, the correct word order is
subject + verb + number of times + time expression.

Past	In 2007, Sana volunteered at the homeless shelter *once a week*.
Present	This year, Sana is volunteering *twice a month*. This year, Sana volunteers *twice a month*.
Present perfect	Sana has volunteered *five times so far*.

Concession clauses with *although* and *even though*

Although and *even though* introduce dependent clauses of concession. Concession clauses give information that is surprising or unexpected compared to the information in the main clause. Concession clauses can come at the beginning or end of a sentence. Use a comma (,) after a concession clause at the beginning of a sentence. Usually you can use *but* or *however* to rephrase a sentence with *although* or *even though*, but the grammar is different.

although / *even though*	*Although / Even though* e-mail is convenient, Mr. Chung doesn't like to use it. Mr. Chung doesn't like to use e-mail *although / even though* it is convenient.
but	E-mail is convenient, *but* Mr. Chung doesn't like to use it.
however	E-mail is convenient. *However*, Mr. Chung doesn't like to use it.

Clauses of reason

Because introduces a dependent clause of reason, which gives reasons or uses for information in the main clause.

Because wireless technology is fast, many people use it.
Many people use wireless technology *because* it is fast.

Adjective clauses with *who* and *that*

An adjective clause comes after a noun. The noun can be in the middle or at the end of the sentence. It can be a person or a thing. *Who* and *that* are used to describe people. Only *that* is used to describe things. There are two kinds of adjective clauses, "subject pattern" and "object pattern."

Subject-pattern clauses

The adjective clause consists of *who* or *that* + verb.
Who or *that* is the subject of the adjective clause.

A camera *that is on sale* costs $99.
I want to buy a camera *that costs less than $100*.

The salesman *who helped me* gave me good advice.
The salesman *that helped me* gave me good advice.

Object-pattern clauses

The adjective clause consists of *that* + noun or pronoun + verb.
That is the object of the adjective clause. In object-pattern clauses you can omit *that*.

I like the car *that you bought*.
I like the car *you bought*.

The mechanic *that I use* has a lot of experience.
The mechanic *I use* has a lot of experience.

Present perfect

The present perfect is formed by *have* or *has* + past participle. One of the uses of the present perfect is to talk about recently finished actions (with or without *just*).
See page 154 for a list of irregular past participles.

Affirmative statements

I You We They	have (just)	cleaned the windows.
He She	has (just)	
It	has (just)	stopped raining.

Present perfect continuous

The present perfect continuous is formed by *have* or *has* + *been* + verb *-ing*. Use the present perfect continuous to talk about actions that started in the past, continue to now, and may continue in the future. Use *for* + length of time to give the meaning of *how long*.

Affirmative statements

I You We They	have been working	for a month.
He She It	has been working	

With verbs that are not actions (e.g., *have*, *be*, *know*), use the present perfect with *for*:
I have known him for two years.
With some action verbs, you can use either the present perfect or the present perfect continuous with *for*: *I have studied / been studying here for six months*.

Participial adjectives

Verb forms that end in *-ed* or *-ing* are called *participles*. Participles can be adjectives. There is a difference in meaning between the *-ed* and *-ing* forms. Often, the *-ing* form describes a thing or person, and the *-ed* form describes the way someone feels.

John's job is very *tiring*. At the end of the day, he is always *tired*.
Mary is at the movies. She is *bored* because the movie is very *boring*.

Connectors of cause and effect

English has many words and phrases to signal cause (reason) and effect (result). Although the meanings of these words and phrases are similar, their grammar is different.

because and *since*	Use these words in dependent clauses to signal the cause. Use a comma (,) when the dependent clause is at the beginning of a sentence. *Because / Since* the earth is getting warmer, the sea level is rising. The sea level is rising *because / since* the earth is getting warmer.
because of and *due to*	These words signal a cause. A noun or noun phrase comes after the prepositions. Use a comma (,) when the phrase is at the beginning of a sentence. *Because of / Due to* air pollution, the children could not play outside. The children could not play outside *because of / due to* air pollution.
therefore, as a result, and *consequently*	These words signal an effect. They come at the beginning of a main clause. They are followed by a comma. The earth is getting warmer. *As a result / Therefore / Consequently,* the sea level is rising.

Conditional sentences

Conditional sentences consist of a dependent clause and a main clause. The dependent clause begins with *if*. Use a comma (,) after an *if* clause at the beginning of a sentence. Conditional sentences can be real or unreal. "Real" means the situation in the sentence is possible. "Unreal" means the situation isn't possible; it is imaginary. In unreal conditional sentences, the form of the *be* verb in the dependent clause is *were* for all persons. The clause *if I were you* is used for giving advice.

Future real conditional

Dependent clause	Main clause	Example
if + subject + present verb	subject + future verb	If I *have* time, I *will bake* a cake. I *will bake* a cake if I *have* time.

Unreal conditional

Dependent clause	Main clause	Example
if + subject + past verb	subject + *would / could / might* + base form of verb	If I *had* time, I *would bake* a cake. I *would bake* a cake if I *had* time.
if + subject + *were*	subject + *would / could / might* + base form of verb	If I *were* you, I *would give* her a gift card for her birthday. I *would give* her a gift card for her birthday if I *were* you.

hope and *wish*

Use *hope* to talk about something you want in the future that is possible. Use *wish* to talk about situations that are not possible (imaginary). Both *hope* and *wish* occur in main clauses and are followed by dependent *that* clauses (see Noun clauses with *that* on page 146).

hope	The dependent clause has a present or future verb or modal. I *hope* (that) you *can come* to my wedding. Sandor *hopes* (that) his son *will fly* home for Thanksgiving.
wish	The dependent clause has a past verb or *would / could* + base form of the verb. I *wish* (that) you *could come* to my wedding. Sandor *wishes* (that) his son *would fly* home for Thanksgiving.

Spelling rules

Spelling rules for gerunds

- Verbs ending in a vowel-consonant pair repeat the consonant before adding *-ing*:
  stop → *stopping*   *get* → *getting*

- Verbs ending in silent *-e* drop the *e* before *-ing*:
  dance → *dancing*   *exercise* → *exercising*
  but:
  be → *being*   *see* → *seeing*

Spelling rules for regular past participles

- To form the past participle of regular verbs, add *-ed* to the base form:
  listen → *listened*

- For regular verbs ending in a consonant + *-y*, change *y* to *i* and add *-ed*:
  study → *studied*

- For regular verbs ending in a vowel + *-y*, add *-ed*:
  play → *played*

- For regular verbs ending in *-e*, add *-d*:
  live → *lived*

Irregular verbs

Base form	Simple past	Past participle	Base form	Simple past	Past participle
be	was / were	been	lose	lost	lost
become	became	become	make	made	made
begin	began	begun	meet	met	met
break	broke	broken	oversleep	overslept	overslept
bring	brought	brought	pay	paid	paid
build	built	built	put	put	put
buy	bought	bought	read	read	read
catch	caught	caught	ride	rode	ridden
choose	chose	chosen	run	ran	run
come	came	come	say	said	said
cost	cost	cost	see	saw	seen
cut	cut	cut	sell	sold	sold
do	did	done	send	sent	sent
drink	drank	drunk	set	set	set
drive	drove	driven	show	showed	shown
eat	ate	eaten	sing	sang	sung
fall	fell	fallen	sit	sat	sat
feel	felt	felt	sleep	slept	slept
fight	fought	fought	speak	spoke	spoken
find	found	found	spend	spent	spent
fly	flew	flown	stand	stood	stood
forget	forgot	forgotten	steal	stole	stolen
get	got	gotten / got	swim	swam	swum
give	gave	given	take	took	taken
go	went	gone	teach	taught	taught
have	had	had	tell	told	told
hear	heard	heard	think	thought	thought
hide	hid	hidden	throw	threw	thrown
hit	hit	hit	understand	understood	understood
hold	held	held	wake	woke	woken
hurt	hurt	hurt	wear	wore	worn
keep	kept	kept	win	won	won
know	knew	known	write	wrote	written
leave	left	left			

Self-study audio script

Welcome

Page 4, Exercise 3A – Track 2

1. Katrina usually cleans her house on Saturday.
2. How long has Samuel lived in Canada?
3. Laura talked to her school counselor yesterday.
4. Mr. Mansour is going to look for a new job.
5. Right now, Andrea is making food for a party.
6. Tony has been working part-time for six months.
7. Last night at 8:00 p.m., the Park family was watching television.
8. We have been waiting for two hours.

Page 4, Exercise 3B – Track 3

Last Monday evening, I was driving home from work when I had a car accident. It was dark, and it was raining. About five blocks from my house, I stopped for a red light. While I was waiting for the light to change, another car hit my car. I guess the driver didn't see me because of the rain. The accident damaged my car badly.

Since the accident, I have been going to work by bus. It's really inconvenient because I work more than 20 miles from my home. The bus is slow, and I have been late several times already. It will take at least two more weeks to fix my car. Until then, I need to find a better way to get to work. I don't want to be late anymore.

Unit 1: Personal information

Lesson A: Get ready
Page 7, Exercises 2A and 2B – Track 4

A Come on in. The door's open!
B Hi, Nina!
A Emily! Come on in. Have you been jogging?
B Yeah, I was just coming back from my run, and I thought I'd see what you're – whoa! Look at this kitchen!
A Yeah, it's a mess, isn't it? We're having 14 people for dinner tonight, and I'm going to be in the kitchen all afternoon!
B It smells great already! Hey, I just heard that Brenda got first place in the high school math contest. Is it true?
A Yes, it's true! She's really good at math. She just loves it.
B Brenda's such a "brain." I'm sure you're really proud of her!
A Yeah, she's very intelligent. But I have to say that Gerry and Danny are bright, too – they're just smart in different ways.

B What do you mean?
A Well, take Gerry. He's not mathematical like Brenda, but he's really musical. He plays four different instruments, he sings really well – he's even writing some of his own songs.
B I guess that's Gerry!
A Yeah.
B So Brenda's gifted in math, and Gerry's good at music. What about Danny? What's he good at?
A Well, he's good at fixing cars. He's the mechanical one in the family.
B Oh, I remember he bought that old, old car when he was 16. How's that coming? Is he still working on it?
A Emily, you should see that car now! It's gorgeous! He fixed everything, and it runs perfectly!
B Amazing! You know, it's really interesting how your kids are all smart in different ways. And, Nina, you're pretty smart, too!
A Me?
B Well, look at you! Maybe it's easy for you to cook for 14 people, but I could never do it. I have absolutely no aptitude for cooking!
A Gee, Emily. No one ever told me that I'm smart!
B Well, Nina, you are smart! And the smart thing for me to do is to go home and let you do your work. I'll talk to you tomorrow.
A Bye, Emily. Thanks for stopping by!

Page 7, Exercise 2C – Track 5

Emily stops by Nina's house on her way home from jogging. They talk about Nina's three children. Brenda is very mathematical. She's just won a math contest at school. When Emily calls Brenda a brain, Nina says that all her children are bright, but in different ways. Gerry isn't gifted in math, but he's very musical. He plays and sings very well and even writes music. Danny is the mechanical one in the family. He's good at fixing up old cars. Emily thinks that Nina is also smart because she is such a good cook. Emily has no aptitude for cooking.

Lesson D: Reading
Page 12, Exercise 2 – Track 6

Many Ways to Be Smart

Josh is a star on the school baseball team. He gets Ds and Fs on all his math tests. His brother, Frank, can't catch, throw, or hit a baseball, but he easily gets As in math. Which boy do you think is more intelligent? Howard Gardner, a professor of education at Harvard University, would say that Josh and Frank are both smart, but in different ways. His theory of multiple intelligences identifies eight different "intelligences" to explain the way

people understand, experience, and learn about the world around them.

Verbal / Linguistic Some people are good with words. They prefer to learn by reading, listening, and speaking.

Logical / Mathematical These people have an aptitude for math. They like solving logic problems and puzzles.

Musical / Rhythmical These people are sensitive to sound, melodies, and rhythms. They are gifted in singing, playing instruments, or composing music.

Visual / Spatial These "picture people" are often good at drawing or painting. They are sensitive to colors and designs.

Bodily / Kinesthetic Some people are "body smart." They are often athletic. Kinesthetic learners learn best when they are moving.

Interpersonal Certain people are "group smart." They easily understand other people. They are good at communicating and interacting with others.

Intrapersonal Some people are "self smart." They can understand their own feelings and emotions. They often enjoy spending time alone.

Naturalist These people are skilled in working with plants and animals in the natural world.

According to Gardner, many people have several or even all of these intelligences, but most of us have one or two intelligences that are primary, or strongest.

Unit 2: At school

Lesson A: Get ready
Page 19, Exercises 2A and 2B – Track 7
Part 1

Do you like to work with people? Do you enjoy traveling? Are you bilingual? Then La Costa Community College's Hospitality and Tourism certificate program is for you. Our graduates find high-paying jobs with hotels, restaurants, airlines, travel agencies, and more! This growing industry needs leaders – it needs you! For more information about La Costa's certificate program in Hospitality and Tourism, call 866-555-6868 today!

Part 2

A Mrs. Ochoa?
B Oh, hi, Vasili. How's it going?
A Pretty well. Um, I was in my car this morning, and I heard an advertisement about a certificate program in hospitality and tourism.
B Yes, it's a great program. Are you interested?
A Yeah, but I have some questions.
B Well, I'll try to answer them for you.

A OK. So first, what are the requirements for the certificate? How many courses are required?

B There are six required courses, plus an internship.

A An internship? What's that?

B You work at a local tourism business for three months. There's no pay, but it's a great way to learn about the industry – you know, see if you like it.

A I see. Are the classes in the daytime or at night? Because you know, I can't quit my job, and . . .

B No problem, Vasili. Classes are scheduled at different times, and some of them are even offered online.

A Oh, yeah? That's great. Um, how long does it take to complete the program?

B Well, it depends. I'd say – with the internship – between one and two years. Some people just take one class at a time, so it takes them longer.

A OK, that's good. How much does the program cost?

B Well, let's see. There are six classes, and they're three units each. It's $20 a unit, so that's $360 for the certificate. Books are another $100 per class, and then there's parking and health fees. So the total is about $1,000.

A A thousand? Wow! That's a lot of money.

B Don't worry. There's financial aid for students who qualify.

A OK. You know, I think I'd like to apply. When's the registration deadline?

B Let's see. Looks like it's December fifteenth for the winter semester. You have time.

A But my English, is it good enough?

B Well, you're required to take an English placement test, but I'm sure you'll do fine, Vasili. You're bilingual, you're very motivated, and you have good interpersonal skills. Hospitality and tourism could be a really good career for you.

Page 19, Exercise 2C – Track 8

Vasili hears a radio ad about the Hospitality and Tourism certificate program at La Costa Community College. The ad says graduates can find high-paying jobs in the tourism industry. Vasili goes to see his ESL counselor, Mrs. Ochoa. She tells him about the program requirements, which include an internship in a local tourism business. She also tells him about the deadline for registration, and she says there is financial aid for students who qualify. Vasili is concerned about his English, but Mrs. Ochoa tells him not to worry. Vasili is bilingual, he's very motivated, and he has good interpersonal skills.

Lesson D: Reading
Page 24, Exercise 2 – Track 9

An Immigrant Family's Success Story

Choi and Lili Wei left China with their baby boy in the late 1980s. They were poor field workers in their native country, and they wanted their child to have the opportunities they lacked. They arrived in New York and found a one-bedroom apartment in a poor, unstable area. They could only afford a bicycle for transportation, yet they felt fortunate to have the chance to begin a new life in the United States.

Choi and Lili faced many obstacles because they couldn't speak English and had no skills. They found night work cleaning businesses and restaurants. They saved every penny, and after six years, they were able to buy a small restaurant of their own.

They were determined to learn English, get an education, and make a good life for their son. The couple sacrificed a great deal. They never went to a movie, never ate out, and hardly ever bought anything extra. In their free time, they attended English and citizenship classes. Both of them eventually earned their GED certificates. Choi then enrolled in college while Lili worked in the restaurant.

This past spring, Choi fulfilled a lifelong dream of graduating from college. Now he is registered in a master's degree program in business beginning this fall. And what about their "baby" boy? Their son, Peter, now 21, received a scholarship to a private university, where he is working on his own dream to become an architect.

Choi and Lili are proud to be models of the "American dream." Choi has this advice for other new immigrants: "Find your passion, make a plan to succeed, and don't ever give up."

Unit 3: Friends and family

Lesson A: Get ready
Page 33, Exercises 2A and 2B – Track 10
Part 1

A You have one new message.

B This call is for Mrs. Wen Lee. This is the attendance office from Central High School calling on Tuesday, March 10th, at 2:00 p.m. We're calling to report an unexcused absence for your daughter, Lan, from her 7th period class today. Please call the office at 619-555-2300 to explain why your daughter missed class. Thank you.

Part 2

C I can't believe we're at the mall on a school day!

D Yeah. Do you think anyone at school is going to miss us?

C No way. There's a substitute teacher in my last period class.

D Mine, too! So, how's everything at home?

C It's the same old thing. I'm so frustrated. My mother won't let me do anything! She is so strict.

D Strict? Like how?

C Well, I'm not permitted to go anywhere without my parents or my brother. And my mom says I can't go out on a date without a chaperone until I'm 18!

D That's so unfair! I wonder why your mother's so strict.

C I don't know. I think she's trying to bring me up like she was raised in China. She just doesn't understand the customs here in the United States.

Part 3

C Hi, Mom.

E Hi, Lan. How was school today?

C Um, fine. Is something wrong?

E The school called and said you were absent from your 7th period class. Where did you go?

C Come on, Mom. Don't get excited.

E Tell me where you went!

C Mary and I just went to the mall right across the street from school, OK?

E But what about your last class?

C There was a substitute teacher, OK? I didn't miss anything!

E I don't understand how you could do this!

C Well, it's your fault! You're so strict that I had no choice. Everybody's allowed to go to the mall except for me. Why can't you trust me?

E This is not about trust. You broke the school rules. You're grounded for the next two weekends.

C Grounded?! What about Celia's birthday party next Saturday?

E I'm afraid you'll have to miss it. Next time, maybe you'll think before you act.

Page 33, Exercise 2C – Track 11

Mrs. Lee received a phone message from her daughter's school saying Lan missed her 7th period class. Lan left school early to go to the mall with her friend Mary. At the mall, Lan tells Mary that her mother is too strict. Lan thinks it's because her mother wants to bring her up the same way she was raised in China. That's why Lan needs a chaperone to go out on a date. At home, Lan and her mother have an argument. Lan is angry because she's not permitted to go to the mall alone. She thinks her mother doesn't trust her. Mrs. Lee is upset because Lan broke the rules. As a punishment, she says Lan is grounded for two weeks.

Lesson D: Reading
Page 38, Exercise 2 – Track 12

Barriers Between Generations

In immigrant families, language differences and work schedules often create barriers to communication between the generations. Dolores Suarez, 42, and her son, Diego, 16, face both kinds of barriers every day. Dolores is an immigrant from Mexico who works seven days a week as a housekeeper in a big hotel. She doesn't use much English in her job, and she has never had time to study it. Consequently, her English is limited. Her son, on the other hand, was raised in the United States. He understands Spanish, but he prefers to speak English. When his friends come over to visit, they speak only English. "They talk so fast, I can't understand what they are saying," says Dolores. To make the situation more complicated, Diego and Dolores live with Dolores's father, who speaks Nahuatl, a native language spoken in Mexico. Diego can't understand anything his grandfather says.

Dolores's work schedule is the second barrier to communication with Diego. Because she rarely has a day off, Dolores isn't able to spend much time with him. She doesn't have time to help him with his homework or attend parent-teacher conferences at his school. In 1995, when Dolores immigrated to the United States, her goal was to bring up her son with enough money to avoid the hardships her family suffered in Mexico. Her hard work has permitted Diego to have a comfortable life and a good education. But she has paid a price for this success. "Sometimes I feel like I don't know my own son," she says.

Unit 4: Health
Lesson A: Get ready
Page 45, Exercises 2A and 2B – Track 13
Part 1

A Cindy, have you seen Sara?
B No. I don't think she's here yet.
A She should have been here 25 minutes ago. Did she call to say she'd be late?
B No, she didn't.
C Oh! Uh, good morning, Mr. Stanley.
A Good morning, Sara.
C I'm sorry, I know I'm late, but the buses are so unreliable.
A I don't know about the buses, Sara, but I do know that if you're late one more time, I'm going to have to fire you.

Part 2

C Thanks for picking me up, Mike.
D No problem.
C We have to hurry – my driving test is in half an hour.

D We have plenty of time. The DMV is just ten minutes from here.
C All right.
D Are you OK? You seem tense.
C Yeah, I'm pretty stressed out.
D How come?
C I was late to work again this morning . . .
D Oh, no!
C And the boss said that if it happens again, he's going to fire me.
D No wonder you're stressed out.
C I'm so worried about losing my job, I can't sleep, I can't eat, I can't concentrate . . .
D You know, Sara, if you're not feeling well, you don't have to take the driving test today.
C Yes, I do, Mike. I have to pass this driving test so I can get my license and buy a car and stop depending on buses.
D OK, OK, I understand. But if you want to pass the test, then you have to calm down. Try to relax. Take a few deep breaths.
C OK.
D Now think positive thoughts. Tell yourself, "I'm a good driver. I'm going to pass my driving test."
C "I'm a good driver, I'm going to pass my driving test."
D Seriously, Sara. You ought to learn some techniques for coping with anxiety.
C Like what?
D Simple stuff. Like I said, deep breathing is good, um, thinking positive thoughts. And I find that it helps me to meditate every day.
C Meditation. Let's talk about it later. Here's the DMV.
D Good luck, and don't forget: You're a good driver!
C Thanks, Mike. You're a good friend.

Page 45, Exercise 2C – Track 14

Mike is driving Sara to the Department of Motor Vehicles (DMV) to take her driving test. He notices that she's very tense. Sara says she's stressed out because she was late to work again. She's worried that her boss will fire her if she's late one more time. She's so afraid of losing her job that she can't eat, she can't sleep, and she can't concentrate. Mike says that she has to calm down if she wants to pass her driving test. He suggests three techniques to help her cope with her anxiety. One is deep breathing. The second one is thinking positive thoughts, and the third one is meditation.

Lesson D: Reading
Page 50, Exercise 2 – Track 15

Stress: What You Ought to Know

What is stress?

Stress is our reaction to changing events in our lives. The reactions can be

mental – what we *think* or *feel* about the changes – and physical – how our body *reacts* to the changes.

What causes stress?

Stress often comes when there are too many changes in our lives. The changes can be positive, like having a baby or getting a better job, or they can be negative, such as an illness or a divorce. Some stress is healthy. It motivates us to push forward. But too much stress over time can make us sick.

What are the signs of stress?

There are both physical and emotional signs of stress. Physical signs may include tight muscles, elevated blood pressure, grinding your teeth, trouble sleeping, an upset stomach, and back pain. Common emotional symptoms are anxiety, nervousness, depression, trouble concentrating, and nightmares.

How can you manage stress?

To prevent stress, you should eat right and exercise regularly. When you know there will be a stressful event in your day – such as a test, a business meeting, or an encounter with someone you don't get along with – it is really important to eat a healthy breakfast and to limit coffee and sugar.

When you find yourself in a stressful situation, stay calm. Take a few deep breaths to help you relax. Roll your shoulders or stretch to loosen any tight muscles. And take time to think before you speak. You don't want to say something you will regret later!

Unit 5: Around town
Lesson A: Get ready
Page 59, Exercises 2A and 2B – Track 16

A Hi! Are you the volunteer coordinator?
B Yup, Steve Jones. And you're Almaz? Did I say it right?
A Yes, exactly, Almaz Bekele. Nice to meet you.
B You, too. Please have a seat. I was just looking over your application to volunteer here at Quiet Palms, and it looks really good. Is it OK if I ask you some questions?
A Of course. Go ahead.
B OK, let's see. You wrote that you've been a volunteer before. Can you tell me about that?
A Sure. I volunteered last summer at the public library downtown.
B What did you do there?
A I worked with adults who wanted to learn how to read. I also taught a little writing, and on Saturdays, I read stories to the kids.
B Did you enjoy that?
A Yeah, but what I really liked was working with the older people. It felt like I was doing something really worthwhile.

B Uh-huh. So now tell me why you want to volunteer in a nursing home.

A Well, I think I might want to work in the health-care field someday, but I won't know for sure until I get some experience.

B I see. Well, we'd love to have you volunteer here.

A Great! When can I start?

B I like your enthusiasm, but we have some health requirements. First, you need to take a blood test and a TB test. You can start as soon as we get the results. It usually takes two or three days.

A OK. I'll take care of that right away. Also, um, I was wondering – can you tell me what my responsibilities will be?

B Sure. One thing volunteers do is, uh, they help residents with their meals. You might encourage them to eat, or just keep them company during mealtime.

A Yeah, my grandmother always eats more when I'm with her. She likes having people around.

B Then I'm sure you understand that you need to be patient and compassionate with the residents.

A I know.

B Volunteers also deliver mail and flowers, and they take residents for walks. You'll get more responsibilities as soon as you feel more confident.

A Sounds good.

B There's an orientation next Monday at 8:30.

A I'll be there!

B One more thing. You'll need to make a commitment to volunteer at least three hours per week.

A No problem! I can't wait to start.

Page 59, Exercise 2C – Track 17

Last summer, Almaz volunteered at the public library downtown. She liked working with the older people because she felt that she was doing something worthwhile. Today, she is meeting with Steve, the volunteer coordinator at Quiet Palms, a nursing home. She wants to volunteer there to find out if she likes working in the health-care field. Steve tells her about some of her responsibilities at Quiet Palms. He says it's very important for volunteers to be compassionate and patient when they are working with the residents. He asks Almaz to make a commitment to volunteer at least three hours per week. Almaz agrees to attend an orientation. She says she can't wait to start volunteering.

Lesson D: Reading
Page 64, Exercise 2 – Track 18

A Worthwhile Commitment

Imagine running with your eyes closed. How do you feel? Insecure? Afraid? Justin Andrews knows these feelings very well. Justin is a former long-distance runner who lost his vision because of a grave illness. For the past six months, he has been running twice a week with the help of volunteer runners at Running with Ropes, an organization that assists blind and visually impaired runners. "Running with Ropes has changed my life," Justin says. "Until I heard about it, I thought I'd never run outside again."

Volunteers at Running with Ropes make a commitment to volunteer two to four hours a week. Scott Liponi, one of the running volunteers, explains what they do. "We use ropes to join ourselves to the blind runners and guide them around and over obstacles, such as holes in the road and other barriers." Scott has learned how to keep the rope loose so the blind runner has more freedom. He deeply respects the blind runners' tenacity. "They are incredibly determined," he says. "It doesn't matter if it's hot, raining, or snowing – they are going to run." Scott says it is gratifying to share in the joy of the runners and to feel that they trust him. "The four hours I spend at Running with Ropes are the most rewarding part of my week," he says. "It's really a worthwhile commitment."

Unit 6: Time

Lesson A: Get ready
Page 71, Exercises 2A and 2B – Track 19

Conversation 1

A Excuse me, ma'am.

B Yes?

A I'm a reporter for KESL Radio, and today we're asking people for their opinions about technology and time-saving devices. Do you have a minute to answer some questions for me?

B Sure.

A May I have your name?

B Jean Rosen. Mrs. Rosen.

A Do you have a favorite time-saving device?

B Let me see. . . . I guess it's this – my address stamper.

A Oh. I expected something electronic, not manual! Does it really save you time?

B Absolutely. It takes about a minute to handwrite a return address. The address stamper just takes seconds, even though it's not electronic.

A Thank you for your time, Mrs. Rosen.

Conversation 2

A Excuse me, sir. Do you have a minute?

C Well, I'm in a bit of a hurry.

A I'm a reporter for KESL Radio. I'm asking people for their opinions about how technology helps them save time.

C Technology – a time-saver? I'm afraid you're talking to the wrong man. I'm not a fan of technology.

A Why is that?

C Well, take e-mail, for example. Half the time it's spam. And it's distracting, too. It interrupts my work.

A But isn't it convenient?

C Not that I can see. If you ask me, most of this electronic stuff wastes more time than it saves. I still write letters by hand, although I have a perfectly good computer at home.

A I see. Could I get your name before you go?

C Ronald Chung.

A Thank you for your time, Mr. Chung.

Conversation 3

A Good morning, ma'am. I'm a reporter for KESL Radio.

D Yes?

A I'm asking people their opinions about technology and time-saving devices.

D Oh, that sounds interesting.

A Do you have a favorite time-saving device?

D Oh, yes. I just love my cell phone.

A I guess it saves you lots of time because you can use it anywhere.

D That's right. You see, I go to lots of sales to buy clothes for my daughter. I take pictures with my camera phone of clothes I think she might like.

A Really?

D Yeah. Then I send her the pictures while I'm still in the store. She sends me a text message back. It says "Buy" or "Don't buy."

A Now that's innovative.

D Yeah. Not a bad idea, huh?

A I'm sure our listeners will enjoy hearing about such an unusual use.

D Happy to share. It really is a time-saver. But not a money-saver.

A I see what you mean! Oh, I didn't get your name.

D Patricia Morales.

A Well, thank you, Ms. Morales, for sharing your favorite time-saving device.

Page 71, Exercise 2C – Track 20

Today, a reporter from KESL Radio asked three people about technology and their favorite time-saving devices. Mrs. Rosen's favorite device is manual. She says it saves time, even though it isn't electronic. Mr. Chung isn't a fan of technology. In fact, he says technology wastes more time than it saves. For example, he says he doesn't like e-mail because he gets lots of spam. He also finds e-mail distracting. He doesn't think it is convenient. Ms. Morales loves technology. She uses the camera on her cell phone in a very innovative way – to send her daughter pictures of clothes that are on sale. Her daughter sends a text message back: "Buy" or "Don't buy."

Lesson D: Reading
Page 76, Exercise 2 – Track 21
Hernando's Blog
Sunday, January 20th

Today, I went with my buddy Rich to a videoconferencing center here in Chicago. It was his birthday, and by using videoconferencing, he was able to have a virtual "party" with his relatives in Guatemala. It was amazing! Rich sat in front of a wide-screen TV here. Meanwhile, his whole family was in front of a screen thousands of miles away, and he could talk to everybody together. I think videoconferencing is an innovative way to keep in touch, even though it's not very convenient. I'm going to find out more about it.

Monday, January 21st

Today, I looked online for videoconferencing centers. Most are for business, so I imagine the costs are outrageous. The center Rich used last night specializes in "reunions" between immigrants and their families in Latin America. First, you have to decide on a date and time. Then, the center here makes the arrangement with a center in the other country. It seems to be pretty popular!

Wednesday, January 23rd

I found out about the costs. The center here charges $40 for a half hour. I think that's reasonable. Luckily, the fee at this center covers the expenses in both countries, so the person in the other country doesn't have to pay anything.

Thursday, January 24th

Well, I picked a date and time for a videoconference with my parents. I want them to meet my fiancée. This is going to be great – I'll be able to see the look on their faces when they "meet" her. Can't do that with a phone or e-mail!

Unit 7: Shopping

Lesson A: Get ready
Page 85, Exercises 2A and 2B – Track 22
Part 1

A Excuse me. Do you work here?
B Yes. Do you need some help?
A Where do I take this thing?
B What have you got there?
A It's a camera, a digital camera. I'd like to get my money back, if possible.
B OK, if you want a refund, you need to talk to somebody in Customer Service. See that guy who's wearing a red tie over there? He'll help you.
A Thank you.
Part 2
C Who's next?
A Hi. I want to return this camera that I bought. I'd like to get my money back.

C You bought it here? Do you have the receipt?
A The receipt? Just a minute. Here it is.
C OK. That's good. Is the camera defective?
A What do you mean – "defective"?
C Well, is there something wrong with it? Doesn't it work?
A Oh, no – it's not broken or anything. I just don't like it.
C What's the problem?
A It's the screen.
C The screen?
A Yeah. The screen is too small. A few days ago, I was taking pictures. It was a sunny day, and I couldn't see the picture in the screen! Maybe it's my eyes.
C No, I don't think it's your eyes. That screen is kind of small. So, did you want to exchange it for another camera?
A I'm not sure. Is it possible to get my money back?
C Well, let me look at that receipt again. You got this on the 5th, and today is the 20th. So it's been 15 days. Our policy for a refund is that you have to bring it back within 10 days. So, sorry – no refund.
A Oh. I didn't know about the 10 days.
C Now, for an exchange: You have 30 days – if the merchandise is in perfect condition.
A Oh, it's just like new! I only used it a couple of times. Here, see for yourself.
C Yeah, you're right. Looks OK to me. Is everything in the box?
A I think so. Like I said, I hardly used the camera. Here's the case that came with it. And here's the instruction book, and the warranty card, and all the papers that –
C OK, great. Why don't I keep this camera here while you look around the store?
A You mean, I have to choose another camera today? I'm kind of in a hurry.
C Well, if you want, I could just give you a store credit instead. With a store credit, you can come back and shop anytime.
A Oh, that's a good idea. Maybe I can bring my nephew with me next time I come. He knows a lot about cameras.
C OK, let me get you a store credit.
A I really appreciate all your help.
C No problem.

Page 85, Exercise 2C – Track 23

Rosa wants to return the camera that she bought and get a refund. She is told that she needs to speak with someone in customer service. The clerk there asks Rosa if the camera is defective. Rosa says that it's not broken, but she doesn't like the screen. The clerk tells her about the store policy for returns and exchanges. It's too late for Rosa to return the camera, but she can exchange it if the merchandise is in perfect condition. Rosa still has the camera box with the instruction book and the warranty card. Since Rosa is in a hurry, she decides to get a store credit, and she will use it at a later time.

Lesson D: Reading
Page 90, Exercise 2 – Track 24
The Smart Shopper
A Dear Smart Shopper,
I'm a jewelry lover, and I enjoy shopping online. Unfortunately, I just bought a pair of gold earrings that I don't like. When I tried to return them, I learned that the seller has a no-return policy. Don't I have the right to get a refund?
— Mad Madelyn
B Dear Mad Madelyn,
If the merchandise is defective, the seller must return your money or make an exchange. However, if the merchandise was in good condition when you received it, and if the retailer has a no-return policy, there is nothing you can do. This is true for store purchases as well as Internet purchases. In the future, here are some questions you should ask before you buy anything:
• Does the seller say "satisfaction guaranteed or your money back"?
• Is there a time limit on returns, such as two weeks?
• Who pays the shipping costs on items that are returned?
• Do you need to return the merchandise in its original package?
• Is the original receipt required?
• Does the retailer give a store credit instead of a cash refund?
• If the retailer has a store in your area, can you return the merchandise to the store instead of shipping it?
Next time, find the return policy on the merchant's Web site and print it, or ask the merchant for the return policy in writing. It's important to get all the facts that you need before you buy!
— Smart Shopper

Unit 8: Work

Lesson A: Get ready
Page 97, Exercises 2A and 2B – Track 25
Part 1

A David. Can I talk to you for a second?
B Yeah, sure.
A Um, you know, you've been leaving early a lot lately, and when you do that, I have to stay later and close up the shop by myself.
B Oh, come on, Yolanda. That doesn't happen very often.
A Well, it happened twice last week, and it's happened once so far this week. I'd say that's pretty often.

Plus, sometimes the shop is full of customers, and you're in the back room talking on your cell phone. So I feel like I've been doing my job and yours, too. It's not fair. Something's wrong here. We have to figure out a better system here so we divide the work more equally.

B OK, whatever – but I have to go now. See you!

Part 2

C Yolanda, over here!

A Hi, guys.

D Whoa, Yolanda – what's wrong?

A I'm exhausted. I've just finished work.

D Don't you usually finish at 4:00?

A Yeah, Teresa; but the other guy on my shift, David, he's going to night school, and lately he's been leaving early a lot. So then I have to clean up the shop and close up by myself. Sometimes I don't get out of there until 4:45 or 5:00. It's really frustrating.

D That's really unfair.

C I think you should quit that job!

D Quit? That's crazy, Julie. She can't quit – it's hard to find another job!

C Well, have you tried talking to David?

A Yeah, I talked to him, but it didn't help.

D What about your boss? Have you told her?

A No, not yet. I'd really like to try to work something out with David first.

C Listen, I have an idea. What about making a chart?

A A chart? How does that work?

C It's simple. You make a list of all the duties in your shift. You know – open up, make coffee, whatever. Then you negotiate with David and decide who's going to do which tasks.

A OK.

C And then, every day, as soon as you finish a task, you write your initials on the chart.

A I get it. So then if David isn't doing his share, it's easy to see.

C And if the problem continues, you can show the chart to your boss and let her deal with it.

A I like that idea, Julie. Especially the part about negotiating with David. I really hope we can work this out together.

Page 97, Exercise 2C – Track 26

Yolanda and David work at Daria's Donut Shop. Lately, David has been leaving work early, and Yolanda has to close up the shop by herself. Tonight, Yolanda is having coffee with her friends. She is exhausted. Her friends give her advice. Teresa thinks she should talk to her boss, but Yolanda wants to try to work things out with David first. Julie thinks Yolanda should make a chart of their duties. Then she should negotiate with David and decide who is going to do which tasks. When they

finish a task, they should write their initials on the chart. If David isn't doing his share of the work, it will show in the chart. Then Yolanda can show the chart to their boss and let her deal with the situation.

Lesson D: Reading
Page 102, Exercise 2 – Track 27
Hard and Soft Job Skills

Som Sarawong has been working as an automotive technician at George's Auto Repair for over five years. Today was a special day for Som, a 35-year-old Thai immigrant, because he received the Employee of the Year award. According to Ed Overton, Som's boss, Som received the award "because he's a great 'people person' and he has superb technical skills. I even have him work on my own car!"

Som has the two kinds of skills that are necessary to be successful and move up in his career: soft skills and hard skills. Soft skills are personal and social skills. Som gets along with his co-workers. He has a strong work ethic; in five years, he has never been late or absent from work. Customers trust him. Hard skills, on the other hand, are the technical skills a person needs to do a job. Som can repair cars, trucks, and motorcycles. He learned from his father, who was also a mechanic. Then he took classes and got a certificate as an auto technician.

Soft and hard skills are equally important, but hard skills are easier to teach and assess than soft skills. People can learn how to use a machine and then take a test on their knowledge. However, it's harder to teach people how to be cooperative and have a good work ethic. George Griffith, the owner of George's Auto Repair, explains, "I've been working in this business for over 30 years, and most of the time when I've needed to fire someone, it was because of weak people skills, not because they didn't have technical abilities." Soft skills and good technical knowledge are a winning combination, and today, Som Sarawong was the winner.

Unit 9: Daily living

Lesson A: Get ready
Page 111, Exercises 2A and 2B – Track 28

A Mei! Dinner!

B I'll be right there! Sorry I'm late. I was just checking something on the computer.

A OK. Sit down. We've been waiting for you.

B I know. I'm sorry, but I was looking at the Web site for this great organization called the Living Green Council.

C "Living green"? What does that mean? I don't even like that color.

B Dad, it means taking responsibility for saving the earth.

C Saving it from what?

B From global warming! We had a guest speaker today in biology class, and he mentioned a whole bunch of stuff – simple steps we can take to reduce our energy use and protect the environment.

A Like what?

B OK, well, first of all, he said we need to cut down on driving, so we should walk, ride a bicycle, carpool, or take public transportation.

C I'd do those things if I could. But my job is an hour away, and there's no bus service that goes there. And there's nobody for me to carpool with.

B I see your point, but how about recycling? I think we could do a better job of recycling bottles, cans, glass, paper . . .

A You're right. We could do that if we tried.

B Another idea was to turn off unnecessary lights. Look at this house: lights on in every room.

C I like that idea. It'll help cut down on the electric bill.

A What else did the speaker suggest?

B Let me think. Oh, he said that we should wash our clothes in cold water.

A Really? I'm not sure the clothes will get clean, but I suppose we can try.

C That'll save money on the electric bill, too.

B But isn't our washing machine really old? If we bought a new one that's more energy-efficient, it could help the environment and our electric bill!

A I don't think we can afford to buy new appliances right now.

B OK. But what about energy-efficient lightbulbs? We could switch to those, right?

A That sounds pretty simple, Mei.

B Cool!

C I have to say, I love your enthusiasm. I never realized how simple it can be to . . . what did you call it . . . "live green"?

B Yeah, the speaker said that if everyone did even one of these things every day, it would do a lot to reduce global warming.

C Speaking of warming, can we eat before the food gets cold?

Page 111, Exercise 2C – Track 29

Mei was late to dinner because she was looking at the Web site of the Living Green Council. "Living green" means taking responsibility for saving the earth from global warming. Mei tells her parents about the guest speaker who came to her class. The speaker suggested simple things people could do to reduce their energy use and protect the environment. For example, they could carpool instead of driving alone, recycle their bottles and cans, and use energy-efficient lightbulbs. Mei's parents agree that it is important to cut down on energy use since it would also help them save money. However, they can't afford to buy new appliances right now.

Lesson D: Reading
Page 116, Exercise 2 – Track 30
All Things Are Connected

Long ago, there was a village chief who never allowed anyone to disagree with him. Whenever he wanted to do something, he asked the members of his court for their advice. But whether the chief's idea was wise or foolish, his advisors always said the same thing: "Indeed, it is wise." Only one old woman dared to give a different answer. Whenever the chief asked for her advice, she always replied, "All things are connected."

One night, the chief was awakened by the sound of frogs croaking in the swamp. It happened again the next night and the next and the next. The chief decided to kill all the frogs in the swamp. When he consulted the members of his court, they replied as usual: "Indeed, it is wise." But the old woman kept silent. "And you, old woman, what do you think?" the chief demanded. "All things are connected," she replied. The chief concluded that the old woman was a fool, and he ordered his servants to kill all the frogs. As a result, the chief slept peacefully.

But soon the mosquitoes in the swamp began to multiply since there were no frogs to eat them. They came into the village and made everyone miserable. The chief ordered his servants to go into the swamp and kill the mosquitoes, but it was impossible. Furious, the chief summoned the members of his court and blamed them, saying, "Why didn't you tell me that killing the frogs would make the mosquitoes multiply and everyone would be miserable? I should have listened to the old woman."

Due to the mosquitoes, all the people of the village were forced to go away. Finally, the chief and his family left, too. Until he died, the chief never forgot the old woman's words: "All things are connected."

Unit 10: Leisure

Lesson A: Get ready
Page 123, Exercises 2A and 2B – Track 31

A Hi, Cathy. What are you doing this weekend?
B Oh, Thanh. I'm glad you asked. I was invited to Bao and An's wedding. It's Saturday night, and I haven't bought them a gift yet.
A So?
B Well, I don't know what to get them. They aren't registered at any stores.

A Registered? What's that?
B Well, for many American weddings, the bride and groom sign up with a gift registry service at a store. They make a list of what they want, and then people can go to the store or the store's Web site and buy something on the couple's list.
A I've never heard of that custom. At a Vietnamese wedding, guests just bring cash in an envelope.
B Really?
A Yeah, and during the reception, the bride and groom walk from table to table, greet the guests, and collect the envelopes. If I were you, I would just take an envelope.
B OK. Thanks for the advice. I guess customs are really different across cultures, aren't they?
A That's for sure. Do you know what really surprised me the first time I went to an American wedding?
B No, what?
A As the bride and groom were leaving the reception, the guests threw rice at them. What a waste of food! Where does that custom come from?
B Oh, that's a really old tradition. Rice is a symbol of fertility and longevity, so throwing rice represents the hope that the couple will have children and live a long life together.
A That's really interesting.
B Yeah. So, Thanh, what else happens at a Vietnamese wedding?
A Well, for one thing, it's traditional for a Vietnamese bride to wear a red dress.
B Red? Not white, like in this country?
A That's right. In our culture, red symbolizes good fortune. In fact, one of the traditional foods at a Vietnamese wedding is red sticky rice.
B Interesting. Let me ask you something else. My invitation was just for the wedding reception in the evening. What about the ceremony?
A Well, traditionally, the ceremony takes place at the bride's home, with just the family and close relatives. It's usually held in the morning. The reception in the evening is actually a huge party, with all the couple's friends and acquaintances, lots of dancing, and lots of food. Be prepared for a seven- or eight-course dinner.
B Wow! I guess I won't eat anything beforehand. So, will I see you at Bao and An's wedding?
A I wish I could go, but I have to go to my nephew's graduation party. I hope you have a great time.
B I hope so, too. I'm really looking forward to it.

Page 123, Exercise 2C – Track 32
Cathy and Thanh are talking about wedding customs. Cathy is invited to a Vietnamese wedding, and she is

surprised that the bride and groom are not registered for gifts at any stores. In contrast, Thanh is surprised by the American tradition of throwing rice at the bride and groom. Next, they talk about clothes. Thanh says a Vietnamese bride wears a red dress because the color red symbolizes good fortune. Then Cathy asks why she was invited only to the wedding reception, not the ceremony. Thanh explains that traditionally the ceremony is only for the family. The couple's friends and acquaintances are invited to the evening reception. In fact, Thanh says the evening party will include seven or eight courses of food. Cathy says she is looking forward to the wedding.

Lesson D: Reading
Page 128, Exercise 2 – Track 33
Special Birthdays Around the World

In most cultures, there are certain birthdays that are especially important in a young person's life. If you were an American teenager, for example, you would eagerly look forward to your 16th birthday because in most states that is the age to get a driver's license. Other cultures also have birthdays with special meanings:

Mexico: For Mexican girls, the 15th birthday – the "Quinceañera" – symbolizes a girl's transition into adulthood. To celebrate, the girl's family throws a huge party. The girl wears a ball gown similar to a wedding dress. The girl performs a waltz, a formal dance, with her father.

China: On a child's first birthday, parents place their baby in the center of a group of objects, such as a shiny coin, a book, and a doll. Then they watch to see which object the baby picks up first. Most parents hope their child will pick up the coin because, according to tradition, it means the child will be rich.

Nigeria: The 1st, 5th, 10th, and 15th birthdays are considered extremely important. Parties are held with up to 100 people. The guests enjoy a feast of a roasted cow or goat.

Japan: A girl's 3rd and 7th birthdays and a boy's 5th birthday are considered special. In a ceremony known as "7, 5, 3," children wear their best kimonos (ceremonial gowns) and receive bags of sweets with "sweets for 1,000 years of life" written on them.

Israel: A boy's 13th and a girl's 12th birthdays are serious as well as happy occasions. On these birthdays, children become responsible for their own religious and moral behavior.

Adult birthdays also have special significance in many cultures. In the United States, for example, birthdays ending in "0" – 30, 40, 50, etc. – are especially meaningful.

Illustration credits

Ken Batelman: 73, 112

Adrian D'Alimonte: 12, 16

Nina Edwards: 9, 37, 46, 89, 133

Chuck Gonzales: 49, 66, 74, 75, 100, 116

Brad Hamann: 38, 64, 87

Ben Kirchner: 6, 18, 32, 44, 58, 60, 70, 84, 96, 98, 110, 122

Monika Roe: 24, 52, 61, 101, 113

Photography credits

1 (*clockwise from top left*) ©1Apix/Alamy; ©Inmagine; ©Jamie Squire/Getty Images; ©Kolvenbach/Alamy; ©Inmagine; ©Inmagine

17 (*clockwise from top left*) ©Hulton Archive/Getty Images; ©Kristian Dowling/Getty Images; ©James Knowler/Getty Images; ©AP Wide World Photo; ©Jennifer Graylock/AP Wide World Photo; ©Hulton Archive/Getty Images

26 ©Jupiter Images

29 (*clockwise from top left*) ©Eric Risberg/AP Wide World Photo; ©Dave Hogan/Getty Images; ©Interfoto/Pressebildagentur/Alamy; ©Charley Gallay/Getty Images; ©Dima Gavrysh/AP Wide World Photo; ©Frank Micelotta/Getty Images

36 ©Jupiter Images

40 (*both*) ©Shutterstock

47 (*left to right*) ©Alamy; ©Inmagine; ©Inmagine

50 ©Inmagine

62 ©Tina Manley/Alamy

69 (*clockwise from top left*) ©Inmagine; ©Inmagine; ©Reuters; ©Inmagine

78 ©Shutterstock

81 (*all*) ©Shutterstock

86 ©Inmagine

88 (*top to bottom*) ©Ryan Nelson/Alamy; ©Shutterstock

90 ©Inmagine

92 ©Shutterstock

102 ©Jupiter Images

107 (*clockwise from top left*) ©Jupiter Images; ©Inmagine; ©Michael Malyszko/Getty Images; ©Frank Pedrick/Jupiter Images

115 (*top*) ©Ron Yue/Alamy; (*bottom, left to right*) ©Daniel Avila/AP Wide World Photo; ©Inmagine; ©Hans Strand/Jupiter Images

118 ©Jupiter Images

124 ©Inmagine

126 ©Inmagine

128 ©Inmagine

130 (*left to right*) ©Newscom; ©Atta Kenare/Getty Images; ©Behrouz Mehri/Getty Images

132 ©Inmagine

X 112773

WITHLACOOCHEE TECHNICAL INSTITUTE
1201 W. Main Street
INVERNESS, FL 34450-4696